Ghetto Child

Chickens and Old Clothes

A World at Twilight

A Portrait of the Jewish Communities of Eastern Europe Before the Holocaust

ART BY Lionel S. Reiss   TEXT BY Milton Hindus

PREFACE BY Isaac Bashevis Singer

WITHDRAWN

The Macmillan Company, New York, New York

COLLIER-MACMILLAN LIMITED, LONDON

The Macmillan Company
866 Third Avenue, New York, N.Y. 10022
Collier-Macmillan Canada Ltd., Toronto, Ontario

Library of Congress Catalog Card Number: 77-156990

First Printing

Designed by Joan Stoliar

Printed in the United States of America

Contents

Preface

BY ISAAC BASHEVIS SINGER

THE JEWS who came to Poland or Russia some eight or nine hundred years ago had greater problems than how to perpetuate their likenesses, their language, their worldly customs, their mode of living. They had fled from countries where Jews as well as Jewish books were burned. They came to territories where half-savage princelings ruled primitive and idol-worshiping tribes. The rulers were in need of merchants, bankers, artisans. The Jews brought civilization to many of these regions. Jews minted coins that had Hebrew letters. They developed trade and industry. They spoke a mixture of Old German, Hebrew, and adopted Slavic words. In their free time they studied the Torah and prayed for the coming of the Messiah. What else was there for them to hope for? A thousand years of exile had convinced them that wherever the Jew builds, he builds on sand. Sooner or later the ghettos, the false accusations, the expulsions were bound to come. To our forebears, life was often an ordeal, a dark corridor where one had to arm oneself with Torah and holy deeds before entering the mansions of Paradise. These preparations, together with the problems of making a living and raising children, occupied them constantly. Recording historical events was not deemed necessary. For the pious Jew the study of history was considered a worldly task, since the past is already in God's hands and in the sphere of His Judgment. Man should concentrate on his holy duties. The painting of portraits and producing works of sculpture were forbidden as acts of idolatry. It is characteristic of those Jews that even though they spent most of their free time studying the Talmud, they had no knowledge of the exact epochs of the *Tannaim* or the *Amoriam* and those who followed them—when and how they lived, in what areas, who preceded whom, and the political and economic situations of their existence. What difference did it make when and how these teachers lived? The only thing of importance was their teachings: what was kosher and what was not, what one was obliged to do and what was forbidden. Biography was a part of worldliness and therefore something for the Gentiles and heretics.

In later years, when the Jews built synagogues and established communities, something of a Jewish style in art emerged. But just the same, the Jews had no ambition to participate in the arts. They didn't mind if an Italian architect came to build their synagogue and designed and built it according to the traditions and styles of his homeland. The essence of a synagogue was not in the walls, the pillars, the lecterns, but in the worshiper's devotion to God and the earnestness of his prayers. The scant history of the Jews of Poland and Russia was gleaned from Responsa, codes of the law, stories of saints. The Chmielnicki massacres produced only one thin volume of tales and eulogies, *Y'vein M'tsulah* ("The Deep Swamp") by Rabbi Nathan Hanover. The Polish historians of later periods ignored the Jews or described them as aliens, enemies, usurers, parasites who must be gotten rid of as soon as possible. Only a few pictures of Jewish life in Poland exist and they were painted by Gentiles.

When Jews in Poland began to print books, a need arose for decorated title pages and illuminations of texts. Jewish goldsmiths and silversmiths fashioned cases for *mezuzahs,* as well as Passover bowls, Torah crowns, pointers, breastplates, spice boxes, esrog containers, and many other ceremonial objects. Jewish brides-to-be embroidered phylactery bags for their bridegrooms, *chalah* covers, and *matzo* holders. This artistry was all connected with religion. Worldly art and worldly literature began among the Polish Jews only in the nineteenth century. Among the first Jewish painters in Poland were Alexander Lesser (1814–44), Maurycy Gottlieb (1856–79), and Leopold Horowicz (1839–1917).

I think I am not exaggerating when I say that Jewish painting in Poland, like Yiddish literature, blossomed in my time. For a few decades there was a wild abundance of talent. Mendele Mocher Seforim, Sholem Aleichem, I. L. Peretz —all died in the twentieth century. I personally knew most of the Jewish painters and sculptors. They were all possessed with the creative urge that had been dormant for many centuries—the need to rescue from oblivion the treasures of our national individuality. So much of it was lost in our history, that what they managed to save was like a drop in the ocean. But even this was destroyed later by the Nazi murderers. Little remained of the works of such artists as the famous Abraham Ostrzego (his monument to I. L. Peretz is still standing in the Warsaw Jewish cemetery), the brothers Zeidenbeitel, Brauner, Barczynski, Apfelbaum, Hirschfang, Friedman, Hanft, Rubinlicht, Kozen, and many others.

Luckily a number of Yiddish artists in Poland and the Soviet Union managed to leave these countries before the Nazi invasion. Some went to Paris, others to Israel; some live and create in the United States of America, like the famous Jacques Lipchitz, Chaim Gross, Raphael and Moses Soyer, and the noted Tully Filmus, Zygmunt Menkes, Ben Zion, Chaim Goldberg, Isaac Lichtenstein, Nathan Hendel, Sol Wilson, Abba Ostrowsky. Among those who saved themselves was the great Yankel Adler, who later died in London.

The wish to eternalize what is transient, to fight the extinction that time and human brutality bring to the individual as well as to the group, is a part of every true artist. But not all artists are aware of it. Among painters and sculptors, just as among writers, there are those who believe that expressions of ethnic nature confine the creator and drive him into clannishness. The artist, they argue, must be universal. He must speak in an international language, a sort of Esperanto of form and color. Actually, those who aspire to such universalism and assimilation never achieve masterpieces. Chagall gained world acclaim only because he remained faithful to Jewish art on his own terms. It is worthwhile to point out that for hundreds of years educated

Russians and Poles spoke French, but they never created a single work of value in their borrowed language. The moment they began to create in Russian and Polish they produced immortals such as Pushkin, Tolstoy, Lermentov, Gogol, Dostoevski, Mickiewicz, and Slowacki. The artist must have a soil. He must have deep roots in his people and his origins. He must be closely connected with the history of his people—their language, customs, beliefs, and superstitions. Great art is often related to folklore. Art must have an address. Those artists who lose their address lose the zest and the juices that nourish their creativity. This is especially relevant in our time when abstraction has been trying to take over art in almost every field. It is the tragedy of the abstract that it has no address. Its address is the human spirit, but that is not precise enough. Abstraction does not spring from a milieu. It has no history, it is seldom connected with a single group. Even when it is clever and inventive, it remains the antithesis of art, which, by its very nature, is attached to time and space, to episodes and visions that can never be repeated, to the details and caprices that the human imagination can never dream up.

Lionel S. Reiss belongs with those rare artists who, early in their lives, became conscious of these truths. Furthermore, he felt that the Jews' very soil and address in eastern Europe were about to dwindle away. During World War I, many Jewish settlements had been wiped out. The Enlightenment, which came to Poland late —about a hundred years later than it came to Germany—rapidly changed the Jewish mode of living. The traditions of hundreds of years disappeared overnight. The Jews in Poland and the whole of eastern Europe changed their attire, their conduct, their way of thinking, their type of education, often even their very language. What was still left had to be artistically recorded by someone. Instead of organizing a movement for this purpose, Reiss decided to do things himself. Almost immediately after the Versailles treaty was concluded, Reiss left his American home and his work as a successful illustrator, and began to wander through the cities and villages of Poland, Galicia, the Ukraine, and Romania. In his quest to discover and set down Jewish ways of life he went to the Holy Land, Egypt, Persia, and many other countries. Changes were taking place among the Jews all over the world. Ruined directly or indirectly by the war, many of them were badly in need of financial help. It was not easy for them to understand why it was so important for someone to paint their poor dwellings, their torn clothes, or the way they washed their linen, fed their babies, carried out their daily tasks at home and at work. From an American visitor they expected help. Reiss had to explain to them that he was not a philanthropist. He himself was poor. He had to clarify for them the purpose of his visit. It seems that the people finally understood him. They posed for him. They did not hide their poverty.

An artist whose purpose it is to document the everyday existence of a people cannot and need not aspire to create masterpieces. He certainly does not need new forms. Experiment is not his aim. One needn't worry too much about form where there is real content. If, in reality, you have a truly interesting story to tell, you need not ponder too much on how to begin and what expressions and effects to use in telling it. Too much concentration on form is symptomatic of lack of observation, of tearing oneself away from nature and from the outside world. During the period when Lionel S. Reiss wandered throughout Europe and the Middle East, the art world was in a mad flurry of experimentation. Expressionism, cubism, and many other "isms" emerged in this period. Many believed that art was sick and tired of describing nature. The aim was to break away from the old forms and find new ones.

9

Lionel S. Reiss was, in a sense, an anachronism. But time has proven—and it will continue to prove more so in the future—that when form is divorced from content and observation, it quickly becomes stale. Art is a synthesis of the inner world of the artist and the world outside. Genuine art is always informative. Art that is shy of the outside world and creeps into its own shell turns solipsistic and narcissistic: it loses its sense. Art is not mere psychology nor a description of psychic states. It must have an object. When it constantly feeds upon its heart or even its brain, it becomes pedantic and obscure. The outside world is full of the unexpected. It is rich in surprises. One can endlessly keep discovering things in it. The inner world is often a mad-house of repetition. It raves more that it tells. It may sound like a paradox, but no one repeats himself more than the one who only indulges in experiments of form and style. His combinations are limited by his very nature. He is bound to fall into mannerisms.

On the other hand, human society, the street, the family, the changes brought about by history contain treasures never to be exhausted. If this is true of all peoples, it is especially true of a people that has been driven from country to country, and even when seemingly settled, never feels completely at home.

More than anyone else, the Jew is unpredictable and full of surprises. He refutes all socio-logical theories, he remains a minority and an exception. It is not an accident that the Jew has become a permanent topic of literature and of art generally. He is a millionaire in individualism. His existence is flux and tension. He is made of such stuff that he feels all the troubles of humanity on his own skin. He has become the meter of human sensitivity. He himself cannot rest and often does not let others rest.

It is good that some of Mr. Reiss's works will appear in a book. Books are not as vulnerable to destruction as paintings and drawings. During World War II, innumerable works of art were destroyed by bombs. What could happen to works of art in the event of an atomic war staggers the imagination. Even the strongest nations could be annihilated. We need many artists like Lionel S. Reiss, who are conscious of the flimsiness and frailty of human existence generally and of our present civilization especially. Nowadays there is no guarantee that New York, Moscow, and London will not share the lot of Warsaw or Kovno. There are moments when one fears that this is almost unavoidable. In a way the whole world can be compared to Poland in the twenties, when Mr. Reiss traveled with his sketchbook and the few belongings that could be carried on a bicycle.

I daresay that long after the trend for the abstract and the many experimentations of our times have become obsolete, humanity will be thirsty for works of art that bear testimony to the life of past generations. In a way this thirst already exists. In the seeming abundance of art we suffer from art-deprivation. The paintings on many of our walls no longer enliven our homes. As for the theater, since it began to shock the audience rather than to describe character, it has become a panopticon of horrors. From its very inception, the film was rarely capable of giving us the artistic enjoyment that we got from good theater, and from the very beginning, television bore the stigma of mass production. Narrative poetry, on which many generations were brought up, has almost disappeared in our time. Story-telling is generally out of fashion. It is becoming more and more a forgotten art. Many novelists hesitate to tell a story directly and simply. Their works often begin in the middle and lack a log-ical conclusion. The short story, which played such an important part in the literature of the nineteenth century, is losing its position. It is slowly being expelled from the magazines. We walk through art galleries and long to see a picture. We sit in the theater and dream about a play that would lift up the spirit; we read a book and yearn for a story and real characters. Many intelligent readers nourish themselves with cheap mystery stories only because they at least contain a plot and suspense even though their characters and situations are contrived.

I approve of the struggle against censorship and I rejoice in its victory, but at the same time I feel that pornography, even at its best, cannot replace literature or good painting. It is lacking in individuality, and is bound to become a cliché. Whenever one reads these miserable books, one reaches the conclusion that they are not really sexy, as are the works of Balzac, Flaubert, or Strindberg. Pornography, like abstraction, has no connection with the time, the group, a way of life. It is merely an extreme expression of the abstract. It does not deal with a definite human being but with the sexes in general. Generalization, whether abstract, symbolic, or pornographic, is the curse of art. The real symbol grows out of the particular. It is the climax of specific events and specific personalities.

True progress in art does not consist of destroying old values. What was once art remains art to the end of time. The nineteenth century was a blessed one, both in art and in science. The rejection of all the gifts of the nineteenth century is a fatal mistake for the artist. The present century is nearing its end. We can already see with dismay that we have not reached and most probably will never attain the accomplishments of the previous one. The artist of the nineteenth century wanted to be loving and truthful; the artist of this century tries to be clever and original. But originality cannot be consciously produced. It stems from an original personality and from the uniqueness that one can find only in the order of events.

Lionel S. Reiss is essentially an artist of the nineteenth century, and because of this he had the power and the courage to tell visually the story of a people. He is a witness to both the decline of the old Jewish way of life in eastern Europe and to the rise of a new way of life, a new cultural orientation. How much richer the knowledge of Jewish history would have been if we could see a likeness of the faces, the garments and the dwellings of the Jews who were captives in Babylon and of those who were permitted to return to their land by Cyrus, king of Persia. Our epoch has many similarities to the one of Ezra. They were felt keenly in the twenties when the Balfour Declaration was looked upon as a sign of the beginning of the redemption, the End of Days. There are both despair and exaltation in the faces that Reiss portrayed. One often gets the impression that these faces had previously existed in our great history. These eyes have seen more than the anxieties and the hopes of our century. They enhance in us the belief in reincarnation. Although it is only forty years ago that Lionel S. Reiss began to draw and paint the Jews of eastern Europe, there is already a scarcity of records of these people. Even good photographs are few. There is no doubt in my mind that for what he has done, Lionel S. Reiss will be remembered, and that those who will write about Jewish life in the eastern Europe of his day, whether history or fiction, will be forever grateful to him for this monument to a vanished people.

In his portrait of the Jewish communities of east Europe before the Holocaust, Professor Milton Hindus presents a historical background to Mr. Reiss' work, which will help the reader conceptualize Jewish life in eastern Europe before Hitler destroyed it. While it was not his intention to supply the reader with a wide and thorough view, which would require many volumes and a lifetime of work, he has brought to the reader's attention vital facts both of religion and secular life in the *shtetl*.

Introduction

A "MEMORIAL BOOK" was published after the Holocaust dedicated to the destroyed White Russian city of Slutzk. In the book there is a significant little footnote that throws a brilliant if indirect light on what it was like to live in that city during the years before war broke out between Germany and Russia in 1941. The note is appended to an article by an American journalist who was the first Western correspondent to see the city after it was recaptured by the Russians in 1944. He describes vividly, from evidence gathered on the spot, both the cruelty and completeness with which the city and its inhabitants were methodically erased soon after it was occupied on the third day of the war. The writer of the note was an American rabbi whose ancestors came from Slutzk. Although he had never been there he had helped assemble the "memorial book."

The rabbi's imagination had been aroused by the tales he'd heard as a child—of the many synagogues and *beth hamidrashim* (houses of study) which had once girdled the square of Slutzk and dominated its landscape of low-slung houses and muddy streets. In particular, his fancy was taken with the name of the town's most famous Jewish house of worship, the so-called *Kalte Shul* or cold synagogue. It took its name from the physical fact that it was just too large to heat properly in the bitter Russian winter and consequently often had to be deserted for months. He asked the correspondent about this and other landmarks, but the latter had seen nothing that could offer a clue about their fate.

Later, the rabbi spoke to a woman who had been an inhabitant of Slutzk and one of the few eyewitnesses to the Nazi occupation who had managed to escape from the city. She clarified quite readily the mystery of what had happened to the *Kalte Shul* and the other synagogues. These well-known edifices serving their original intentions and purposes had existed, unfortunately, only in the imagination of the rabbi for many years prior to the time that the Germans had come. All the synagogues of Slutzk had long before been taken over by the Soviet government and used for secular purposes. In particular, the great *Kalte Shul* had been used as a bakery since the 1920s! The younger generation either had never known or else completely forgotten the connection between these buildings and the Jewish religion! The Holocaust had given the *coup de grâce*, in this instance, to a way of life that had been gravely wounded and weakened long before, and the nostalgia of the children of those who emigrated to America from the Czarist Pale of Settlement must attach itself, therefore, to a period prior to the Bolshevik Revolution of 1917.

WARSAW, THE POLISH REPUBLIC, AND RUSSIA

In fact, as one learns from I. B. Singer's *The Family Moskat*, the metamorphosis in the traditional life had set in long before—specifically with the abortive Russian Revolution of 1905. Speaking of the city of Warsaw, which before World War I was under Russian rule, Singer notes the effect of that traumatic event in the numbers of Hasidic youth on the streets of the city who had cast off their traditional costumes: long black caftans, fur-trimmed *streimels* on their heads, white stockings, unshaved *payith* (or curls about their ears). Some of them had even become factory workers, socialists of one kind or the other, or Zionists. Some girls from perfectly conventional families absconded with university students to the United States, South America, or Palestine. More matrons than before discarded the *sheitel* (or plastered-down wig, which a girl was expected to assume when her own hair, having served its purpose, was cut off at the time of her marriage according to immemorial religious custom). Those interested in finding scapegoats to blame for these defections, which were so shocking, were inclined to attribute them to the subversive modernistic tendencies in much of the Yiddish literature and pamphleteering of the period.

The hopes of the modernists, however, were destined to be as savagely disappointed in the new Republic of Poland, which came into existence in November, 1918, as in the Soviet Union, which began its checkered revolutionary career a year before. In the "new" Poland—as a journalist was to explain in 1926—it was not merely a fact that the Poles hated the Jews emotionally. Their resentment was rationalized by their ambition to build up as pure a Polish civilization as possible. Jews—especially middle-class and professional Jews—stood in the way of the realization of this ideal. Symptomatic of that period was the trial of a Jewish woman physician on a charge of changing her Jewish name to a Polish one. The new Polish constitution presumably guaranteed Jews equal rights—even the right to change their names if they wished—but the government produced an old Czarist law forbidding Jews to be known under any but Jewish names and subjected this ancient chestnut to a test in the Polish Supreme Court. Although the court's decision sustained the woman and the law was declared unconstitutional, the administrative arm of the government refused to recognize the ruling of the court. It is not very difficult to imagine how this affected the psychological security of the Jewish community.

Subsequently, Jews were as systematically squeezed out of professional and public life as decency of appearance permitted. What has come to be called "tokenism" was, of course, not unknown. Jewish professors—who could be numbered on the fingers of one hand—were permitted to teach in the universities, but they were the exceptions that proved the rule. Many Jewish students were admitted to the universities, but they faced blind alleys when they graduated. Not only was the teaching profession closed to them (with the exception of a few Jewish schools), but also almost all engineering, law and civil service. A military career, it goes without saying, was not even to be dreamt of. The excuse given for these exclusions was the inadequate command of the Polish language by the Jews. This was something less than the truth. Whatever had been true in the old days, the new generation of Jews in Poland knew Polish better than it did Yiddish. The Poles also accused Jews of a lack of patriotism or, as they put it, Jews "have no solidarity with the Polish state." But they failed to explain why Jews could be expected to have patriotic feelings toward a government that discriminated against them, or indeed what standards they were applying to arrive at their judgment. Some noted cynically that a Pole must show only ordinary loyalty, but a Jew must give evidence of at least ten times as much if he aspired to consideration as a servant of the state.

The Polish government's anti-Semitic attitude was especially influential because its sphere of economic activity was so large. The government operated the railroads, and the production and sale of tobacco, alcoholic beverages, matches, and salt were all state monopolies. Almost no Jews were employed on the railroads, and when the tobacco and alcoholic-beverage industries were nationalized, almost all the Jewish workers, who had been employed when these were privately owned, were dismissed. Two tobacco factories, which, under private ownership, had employed almost nine hundred Jews between them, gave employment to only five Jews after the state took them over. In another case, in which 95 per cent of the "hands" before nationalization were Jewish, the number dropped to 6 per cent after the Polish state took over.

With so many avenues closed against talent or even the willingness to do work of any kind, it is not surprising that Jewish Polish youths of the late 1920s were described by some travelers and observers as dispirited and lackadaisical. The boys often became *luftmenschen* and speculators of various kinds. The girls sat at home waiting for husbands. Typical Warsaw young people who had nothing better to do in the evening loafed around cafés, where they left an unfortunate impression upon foreigners. The boys seemed pale-faced and half-grown, and they were dressed in poor imitations of well-tailored suits. The girls were sad and empty-eyed, and the dancing couples moved around the floor to the tunes of second-rate jazz with neither ecstasy nor any visible enthusiasm. They had little to be happy about. The boys could wait for their fathers to die so that they might enter the economy as small businessmen, faced with ever-shrinking opportunities because of the attitudes of the society around them and of the government. The girls had even fewer prospects as they sought to interest these wilted young men in themselves.

Yet Polish Jewry between the two world wars, although tragic in its plight, was in some respects better off than its Russian counterpart across the border. In Poland, Hasidim may have had to fear the taunts of street hooligans who occasionally did not scruple to pull them by their beards or make them yield their places in conveyances such as streetcars; but at least they did not face organized campaigns by the government against all religion as in Russia. And though the generation gap in Poland was certainly not small, it was not sharpened by fanatic politicians in power who deemed it a victory to split apart each family and to set up the children to act as informers against their parents. Indeed, in Poland, up to 1939, Hasidim gathered in such substantial numbers at certain times of the year for pilgrimages to the Rabbi of Ger and other spiritual potentates that the government, despite its distaste for them, felt compelled to schedule extra trains to accommodate them.

In Russia, where all organized efforts to perpetuate religious traditions were viewed with jaundiced eyes by the Bolsheviks, such gatherings would have been attended by suspicions of conspiracy against the regime. All religions were equally discouraged, but in this respect the Jews were, in George Orwell's words, "more equal" than the others. Long before the latent anti-Semitism of the Soviet dictator Stalin surfaced during the struggle against Trotsky, many Russian Jews had been caught in an economic as well spiritual whipsaw. According to an astute independent observer of Soviet life, of the three million Jews in the Soviet Union in the middle 1920s, one third were employed in industry, government service, or farming; one third eked out a meager living as independent hand-workers; and one third still pursued increasingly precarious business vocations, shunting from one thing to another, uncertain of the future and racked with fear of ever more restrictions imposed upon them for belonging to the despised nonproletarian segment of society. Jewish Communists, most of whom were not yet disillusioned by the growing discriminations against them, declared open season on their coreligionists and did everything they could to force assimilation, which proposed a solution of "the Jewish problem" through a dissolution of the Jewish people. At the end of the 1920s, a writer on Russia concluded that the Jews, one way or another, were destined for complete assimilation under the Soviets. More than thirty years later, the same writer had to admit that he could not have been more wrong in his prediction. What took place within this period were, of course, the war, the Holocaust, and the establishment and preservation of the state of Israel. The consequences of these events could hardly have been foreseen by anyone.

PRAGUE AND KAFKA

A third perspective or aperture into the mysteries of the east European mind before the Holocaust is offered by a writer who lived at the westernmost periphery of it, Franz Kafka. Kafka lived in Prague, first under the Hapsburg monarchy and then under Masaryk's Czechoslovak Republic. He was a native speaker and writer of German; later he learned Czech. Thus he seemed to have not one but two escape hatches open to him if he wanted to get away from his Jewish identity. But, as is well known, he did not avail himself of the possibility. And though he never became a Zionist, as did his friend and biographer Max Brod, and never managed to catch hold, as he put it, of "the flying prayer-shawl of the Jews," he was obsessively if ambivalently drawn back again and again in the direction of his Jewish origins until his death in 1924, when he was engaged in a serious study of Hebrew. Before that, he had studied Yiddish and its literature and made himself a conspicuous defender of that language, which has so often been patronized by the very people who have used it most. One statement of his in particular has been quoted many times: "I would tell you, ladies and gentlemen [this was the introduction to a lecture], how much better you understand Yiddish than you think."

The roots of the Prague ghetto go deep into history. Mention of Jews in the city can be found before the year 1000, and there are references to its Jewish cemetery in the middle of the thirteenth century. In the sixteenth century, it was the location of the activities of the legendary Golem. But after many persecutions, expulsions, and vicissitudes, by the end of the nineteenth century and the first quarter of the twentieth century, the community seemed well on the way to voluntary submersion and union with the surrounding world. And it was against this assimilatory tendency that Kafka was moved to protest eloquently in his well-known "Letter" to his father. Here Kafka speaks not only for himself but for all those in the modern world, who, in being given a watered-down version of an older and more impressive tradition, feel that they have been robbed by their parents of some portion of their Jewish, indeed human, patrimony. Kafka in this missive touches upon the difference between provincial east European Jewishness, which he obviously regards as the authentic kind, and the city-bred modern simulacrum of that way of life, which has been compromised somehow by the effort to bring it into line with the ways of the world. Kafka speaks to his father plaintively of his childhood memories of what is to most other Jews the most gloriously remembered of holidays, "the first Seder night, which always turned rather into a comedy with fits of laughter, brought about it is true by the influence of the elder children." And he asks his father accusingly: "Why did you have to give in to this influence?" and immediately answers his own question: "Because you yourself had produced it, of course."

Kafka then goes on to trace rather understandingly and persuasively how that particular point in the degeneration of a venerable tradition had been reached by his father: "You really did bring something of Judaism with you out of your tiny little ghetto-like country parish; it wasn't much, and a little of that got lost in the city and in the army, but all the same there was just enough left of impressions and memories of youth to satisfy your kind of Judaism, particularly as you didn't need much help of that kind, seeing that you came of a very sturdy stock, and, as far as you were concerned, could hardly be shaken by religious doubts unless they got mixed up too much with social doubts. . . . But as far as your child was concerned, it was not enough to be passed on, it trickled away drop by drop as you

tried to hand it on. . . . It was impossible to make a child driven to overcritical observation by sheer fear understand that the few insignificant details you performed in the name of Judaism, with an indifference which matched their insignificance, could have a higher meaning. For you they had a meaning, as little memories of old times, and that is why you wanted to hand them on to me, but could do so, since they had no more intrinsic value for you yourself, only by persuasion or threats, that could not succeed, on the one hand, and on the other hand, couldn't fail, since you didn't realize the weakness of your position in this matter, to make you furious with me for what you thought was my intransigence."

Later efforts on Kafka's own part to repair the early omissions in his religious training were without avail. Like other young intellectuals of his generation, he tried to find his way back to an appreciation of an ancient tradition, but he was basically too honest to flatter himself with the notion that he had succeeded. Max Brod tells us that Kafka once accompanied him to a so-called "Third Meal" at the end of a Hasidic Sabbath, with its characteristic whispering and chants, but remained cool and unmoved. Later, Kafka said to his more responsive friend: "If you look at it properly, it was just as if we had been among a tribe of African savages. Sheerest superstition."

So, like many another modernist, he was torn by the conflict in himself between desire and assent. He was drawn simultaneously in opposite directions, and his intellect and eloquence enabled him to speak lucidly on behalf of many who could not speak for themselves. It was not the least of the ironies surrounding the tragedy of the Holocaust that many who perished must have gone to their doom (as he himself might have gone had he not been cut off prematurely by the disease of tuberculosis) with all of the ambiguities of attitude that characterized Kafka side by side with legions of caftaned Hasidim of the kind he had looked at unsympathetically that Sabbath day.

We know what Kafka's feelings were precisely because he was able to give expression to them and because that expression was entirely adequate. If only we knew more about the feelings of many others in the same way, we should not have to grope in the dark trying to find answers to our questions about this relatively recent period of history. The philosopher Schopenhauer was right when he remarked: "Nations are really mere abstractions; individuals alone actually exist!" And so was Marcel Proust when he wrote in the same vein: "People foolishly imagine that the vast dimensions of social phenomena afford them an excellent opportunity to penetrate further into the human soul; they ought, on the contrary, to realize that it is by plumbing the depths of a single personality that they might have a chance of understanding these phenomena."

Origins

THE PLAYWRIGHT S. N. Behrman, born and brought up in the city of Worcester, Massachusetts, gathered impressions, like a child in every other immigrant home, of the east European background from which his parents had emerged. Behrman's feeling, as he delineates it in his memoir, *The Worcester Account,* was of the chasm that separated that home from everything else he experienced in his everyday life outside it. Home was where the embarrassing "dialect" Yiddish was spoken; it was also the scene of what he calls the Great Theater. What he means by this description—in addition to its ironic overtones implying a kind of sentimentality and melodrama at odds with the coolness and restraint characteristic of the "Yankee" environment—is that various biblical and legendary personages were referred to so familiarly in the language of his parents as to create a conviction of their immediate reality and nearness in space and time.

That conviction was part of the heritage carried over from the old country, where, of course, it was much stronger than it could ever be in America. One of the most popular biblical characters about whom a mass of legend and folk tales gathered was Elijah, who according to popular belief, never died and even now comes frequently to visit those Jews who are deserving and in need of his presence—which is unfortunately, guessed at only after he has gone, leaving nothing but a cloud behind him. So deep was this belief in the visitations of Elijah among east European Jews, that during the ceremony attending the circumcision of a male child, a special chair was left vacant for the use of the good prophet. Even better known than this custom was the one that called for the setting aside of a special goblet of wine for Elijah during the Passover *seder;* and the children strained their eyes at the moment tradition called for him to appear in order to catch the slightest trembling on the surface of the wine as he deigned to touch it with his invisible holy lips.

Nor was Elijah the only one who walked the earth of eastern Europe. Moses and David on occasion left the heavenly sphere, too, in order either to help believers or restrain them if they were in peril of abandoning the righteous way

19

and falling into sin. King David himself was supposed to preside over that meal at the conclusion of the Sabbath which excited the skepticism of Kafka, for it was then that there was a song in which his name was mentioned. The repast was known as *mlave-malke,* and it was said that King David used to appear to celebrants when they were unusually troubled. He was known by his retinue of courtiers and musicians, as well as by the harp he held in his own hands. It was expected that if necessary he would employ supernatural means to aid his devotees.

It has been remarked, with reason, that the east European Jews were inordinately fond of storytelling. They would stay up late at night, particularly in the winter, passing the time away with a ceaseless flow of stories. A stranger who was adept as a storyteller was certain of a good welcome wherever he went. Wandering beggars, transient Yeshivah students, and tailors enjoyed particularly fine reputations as purveyors of tales. These tales were by no means all Jewish but came from a variety of sources. In fact, folklorists seem to be in agreement that Jews were most important in the spread of folk literature in the Middle Ages. They were the natural carriers of such stories from west to east and back again. Storytelling has continued to be one of the most durable of Jewish traditions. When modern Yiddish literature began in the middle of the nineteenth century, one of its early successes was a Jewish version of *Don Quixote* by Mendele Mocher Seforim in which the protagonist loses his reason from pondering too long upon the wonder-tales of the River Sambation (which was tumultuous and loud all week long but piously rested on the Sabbath). He set out in quest of the strange race of men who were said to live on the other side of the Sambation River, though he never actually managed to get beyond Berdichev.

The attempt to trace the ultimate origin of anything in this world, as Thomas Mann suggests in the *Joseph* stories, is likely to prove a chase after a will-o'-the-wisp that leads to depths within depths. It is a baffling, frustrating quest that in the end is self-defeating. History is a seamless web, and the decision to cut into it at any particular point must necessarily be an arbitrary one. The unmistakable German base of the Yiddish language common to the Jews throughout eastern Europe suggests their ultimate origin in western Europe, but it is hardly necessary here to try to trace the steps by which they first came there and merged with and ultimately dominated culturally whatever Jews may have been indigenous to the Slavic regions. By the beginning of the sixteenth century, we are told, substantial numbers of Jews stemming from the Middle Rhine were settled in compact groups in towns and cities in Bohemia, Poland, and Russia, the rulers of which had apparently admitted them with the express purpose of forming the nucleus of a town population among the predominantly agricultural Slavs.

These Jews in eastern Europe for a long time evidently had nostalgic longings for the old scenes in the west from which they were now distant. Thus when the legends about the Nibelungen, Siegfried, and King Arthur began to go out of fashion and favor in other parts of Europe, they continued to live on among the Jews in the Slavic countries and to give enjoyment there. They can be found in the so-called *Maasebuch* (storybook), the author of which apparently was a native of Meseritz in Lithuania. It was probably to infiltrate, to supplement, or to counteract the popularity of such non-Jewish materials that the Jewish religious leaders introduced more specifically Jewish legends in such popular works as the *Tzenou u'renou,* which served many generations of Jewish women (and men too humbly placed in the social order to receive a thorough Hebrew education) by translating the weekly "portion" of the Pentateuch into Yiddish and commenting and embroidering fancifully upon it.

The original name "Yiddish" (that is to say, the language of the Jews) was *Teutsch,* and philological reminders of that old designation survive to this day in such Yiddish words as *verteutschen* (meaning to translate, that is, to do into German) and, more surprisingly, in the word *steutsch* (the equivalent of "How do you mean it?"), which appears to be a contraction of *is teutsch* or "How is that in German?" Of course, this Germanic element in the Yiddish language has, in the course of time, been interfused with Hebraic, Slavic, and other linguistic elements, and it is written in Hebrew characters and pronounced very differently from modern German. But the Germanic origins of Yiddish remain clearer perhaps than do the Germanic origins of the English language.

The Yiddish language was preserved in its pristine state for centuries by the conditions of isolation and autonomy under which the Jewish communities of Poland and Russia lived. It was only toward the middle of the nineteenth century that barriers against the participation of Jews in Russian culture appeared about to be lifted. Sufficient numbers of Jews responded positively enough to the beckoning opportunities to inspire assimilationists with the hope that, had the atmosphere of liberalism and tolerance lasted only a little longer, Yiddish literature would have faded into the past. However, the assassination of Alexander II in 1881 by the Nihilists and the pogroms and reaction that followed completely altered the situation. The tide toward Russianization was reversed. Jews were driven back into themselves. National consciousness among them revived; forms of proto-Zionism appeared; and all things that served to mark them out as an independent people (such as speaking a language of their own) were strengthened. Some who seemed to be on the way to making a career in Russian letters, like Simon Frug, were shocked into returning to their mother tongue. In 1879, Frug began to publish poems in the Russian language. But after the terrible events of 1881 (the killing of the liberal Czar by revolutionaries and the reaction, of which the Jews were the first victims), he began (in 1885) to publish in the Yiddish language.

Assimilationists, universalists, believers in the irresistible powers of progressive enlightenment and civilization felt on this occasion, as they had before and would do again, that they had come very close to the realization of their dreams of making the Jews "come out of their shell" and mingle freely with mankind. But it was to prove once again a case of "so near and yet so far." Between the roseate Utopian "ideal" and the reality of everyday existence there fell the shadow of the periodic persecution that had been the lot of dispersed Jewry in general and east European Jewry in particular over millennia. An enforced separatism (either crude or subtle), at what seemed to the eternally hopeful the eleventh hour, received a reprieve from extinction.

Primitive
Living Conditions

I
N HIS MEMOIRS, Maurice Samuel asserts
that "the Jewish attitude toward the
shtetl was and is ambivalent." It had one
foot in the age of faith and the other in
the age of wood. It provided the social animal in
man with a welcome form of spiritual security
but exacted a price of conformity in return that
was occasionally exorbitant. It was a prime
instance of the validity of William Blake's
observation:

Do what you will, this world's a fiction
And is made up of contradiction.

Whatever sentimentalists or latter-day pietists
may claim, it was a bundle of paradoxes and
ambiguities, like all living organisms. It was, if
you like, an accident of history fated to perish
in an unparalleled catastrophe. But then, to
quote Saul Bellow, "we are all such accidents."
At times, it is true, the sequence seems anything
but accidental, and we may suspect the working
of providence in the concatenation of events. In
an age of doubt, we still have twinges of faith.
But whatever the comforts we derive from this
"antiseptic of the soul," decisive evidence is lacking with which to refute Bellow's existentialist
conclusion that "We do not make up history and
culture. We simply appear, not by our own
choice. We make what we can of our condition
with the means available. We must accept the
mixture as we find it."

The "mixture" that most immigrants who
later wrote about it remembered was hardly
pleasant to the taste. In making the long journey
to America (in steerage, for the most part) they
felt that they had crossed not merely vast areas
of geographical space but of social time as well.
Traversing the distance between medieval and
modern times in a few short weeks was an experience for some comparable to that of a diver
being catapulted from the lower depths of the
ocean to a surface full of light and air. Not surprisingly, it produced on occasion a spiritual
phenomenon not unlike the physical one known
as "the bends," which may prove fatal. A writer
who came from a family of *yishuvniks* (that is to
say, Jews who were scattered and isolated among
the peasants in remote country villages of Russia) recalls that his mother gave birth to all
eleven of her children in the straw on the floor,

with no doctor, no *feldsher* even, no midwife in attendance—only an old *muzhik* woman who lived across the way, a *babka* who knew nothing of hygiene or sanitation and cut the umbilical cord with a kitchen knife that she wiped on her apron. Another writer who came from a larger Jewish settlement remembers her grandfather's house as a small one-story wooden building that stood flush with the unpaved street. It had a yard with a gate so high off the ground that four-footed visitors, which included squealing pigs, did not have to wait till it opened to enter. Still other Jews remembered sheltering livestock in their own dwellings in the wintertime.

A typical Jewish town was located at some distance from a railway station. It had neither factories nor large-scale industry to bolster its economy. It subsisted, after a fashion, on trade with peasants who brought their produce from field and forest and exchanged it for such goods as shoes, nails, kerosene, salt, and linens. The houses were likely to be built of partly-planed logs with moss between them, and it was a rare house that had a wooden floor instead of hardened earth. The huts of the surrounding peasants were still simpler constructions, made of logs put together to form a cone with an opening left at the top for the smoke to come out. Inside, the atmosphere was heavy with smoke, for in the center there was a fire that burned night and day. During the day it was used for cooking, in the night to keep warm. Around it, the peasants and their families slept in their clothes, using their overcoats as cushions.

It was a fortunate town that was located on the banks of a river, since the most serious lack felt in a town was an inadequate water supply. The water usually came from a few wells or ponds, and the inhabitants were still largely dependent upon the water-carrier, from whom they bought such supplies as they were unable to provide by such methods as gathering rainwater with pots and pails. As a rule, women bore a disproportionate amount of the burdens, for which they received minimal credit. Not only were the families large, but they had to run or help to run such business as there was. They chopped wood, baked bread, and, when the water-carrier was not available or they wished to save the expense, they had to travel long distances to fetch water, and carry it uphill and along unpaved streets proverbial for their icy slipperiness in the winter and for their ankle-deep mud in the spring. In the winter, if there was a river a mile away, the washing of tablecloths, bed sheets, and underwear sometimes had to be done through a hole in the ice. A kind of primitive wooden mallet was used in conjunction with a washboard to hammer and wring the water out of the freezing wet-wash.

A short water supply was naturally accompanied by frequent fires, especially in the summer. Fire-fighting brigades and insurance were unknown. One immigrant writer wryly recalls that every time the weekly portion of the Pentateuch began with the Book of Numbers, chapter eight: "Thou shalt kindle . . . ," everyone in town expected a fire. When such fears were realized, there was nothing better to do than gather as many of one's belongings as could be managed, carry them into the fields, and hope for the best. After such a description, it hardly needs to be added, that the town contained no places of public amusement such as theaters or dance halls. Life centered on the *shul* (or synagogue) and the *beth hamidrash* (which is usually rendered as "house of study"), where all the needs, not only of devotion but for distraction, had to be satisfied.

The costumes that people wore—gaberdines, headgear, visible fringes of the *talith katan* (or short prayer-shawl)—had been settled by tradition centuries before. A man in the dress of the middle of the seventeenth century would have caused no comment in the same place two hundred fifty years later. Styles of hairdo, of course, are notoriously uneven in their development, and conflicts did arise over them at times. One immigrant writer tells us that when he returned to the city of Minsk from the town of Neshwies, where he had been brought up by his rigorously pious grandfather, his *payith* (or locks of hair grown luxuriantly about the ears) made him a laughingstock. His own sister teased him about the queer ways he had developed during his three-year absence from the big city.

Furnishings were simple, but copper candelabra hanging from the ceiling, satin-covered pieces of furniture, and heavy oak bookcases generously filled to overflowing with volumes of varying sizes were not unknown. In fact, according to Professor Heschel in *The Earth Is the Lord's,*

> in almost every Jewish home in eastern Europe, even in the humblest and the poorest, stood a bookcase full of volumes, proud and stately folio tomes together with shy, small-sized books.... Almost every Jew gave of his time to learning, either in private study or by joining one of the societies established for the purpose of studying the Talmud or some other branch of rabbinic literature. To some people it was impossible to pray without first having been refreshed by spending some time in the sublime atmosphere of Torah. Others, after the morning prayer, would spend an hour with their books before starting to work. At nightfall, almost everyone would leave the tumult and bustle of everyday life to study in the *beth-ha-midrash.*

There is some difference of opinion among writers on eastern Europe as to how much class-consciousness existed in the Jewish small town, but there is evidence to support the contentions of those like Professor Heschel, who see in the universal love of learning that characterized the *shtetl,* a leavening and democratizing influence upon its social structure. Heschel cites one striking instance, an item that turned up at YIVO (the Yiddish Scientific Institute) after World War II bearing an inscription identifying it as the property of a "Society of Woodchoppers for the Study of the Talmud" in an unknown provincial little place in eastern Europe.

It would be a mistake, of course, to exaggerate or sensationalize the sheer physical novelty and wonder aroused by the sight of America in the immigrants. It depended largely on where they had come from. The one who came from Minsk confessed to feeling disappointed when he found that the largest avenues of the old East Side of New York were not more impressive than the great business streets, such as the Franciscaner, with which he was familiar. And had he come from a still larger city like Kiev (in which, before World War I, Jews had had to obtain special privileges to dwell) and known its famous and beautiful thoroughfare the Kreshchatik, he might have been still more disillusioned. But if he had come from a smaller and more representative township in the Pale of Settlement where a large part of the Jewish population (outside of Poland) was concentrated, his reaction would have been quite different. Many an immigrant remembered all of his life (or her life) the profound shock that the initial glimpse of millions upon millions of flickering lights in a megalopolis had produced upon his mind.

Old Scribe

Lomza Courtyard

Lublin Tower

27

Inner Court, Lodz

Rowne Backyards

Stanislav Passageway

Hallway, Kamieniec

Breadline, Warsaw, 1921

Krakow Shops

Rabbi Meisel's Passage, Krakow, East

Galician Fair

Tarnopol

Glasser Street, Vilna

Prayer Books and Prayer-shawls

Market in Chelm

Yavarov Courtyard

Romanian Ghetto

43

The Wanderer

Ghetto Alley

Alley and Synagogue, Vilna

46

Ulica Josepha, Krakow

Interior

Krakow Homes

Occupations,
Poverty,
Mutual-Aid Societies

"INERTIA IS THE first law of history as well as of physics," wrote Morris Raphael Cohen, who had been born in eastern Europe. This could have been a conclusion arrived at by observing that world right up to World War I and the Russian Revolution, and (some would say) from observing it afterward as well. The more things change, the more they remain the same, is a saying that highlights its opposite—that Heraclitean vision that perceives reality as an unceasingly changing flux and experience as a perpetual gushing forth of novelties. The infamous Pale of Settlement disappeared with the Czar only to be succeeded by the famous *fifth point* on the identity card that every Soviet citizen carries and that identifies its bearer as belonging to the Jewish "nationality" (which in the Soviet Union has none of the privileges of other recognized nationalities) whether or not he or she wishes it. And today, as under the Czar, Soviet law does not permit change of name or nationality. That so-called "fifth point" has been described as the bane of Soviet Jewry, which, though presumably never intended as such, has in practice proved

a discriminatory measure so crippling that cynics now speak of the passport as certifying "fifth-class invalidism."

During the time of the gifted historian Dubnow, who perished at the hands of the Nazis in his eighty-first year in the city of Riga in 1941, the situation of the Jews in eastern Europe had seemed so stable (some said stagnant) over a long period of time that he was encouraged to suggest the renewal or preservation of Jewish autonomy in eastern Europe as a practicable political goal to be pursued in the twentieth century. At first, this aim would seem to have been as realistic as the slogan of self-determination for the American Indian. But sympathetic examination reveals that Dubnow's view was not simply the outgrowth of nostalgia for a political situation that had actually prevailed in Poland centuries before but a more sober judgment based on his conclusions about the self-sufficiency and spiritually resistant character of the Jewish communities that he had studied and with which he was familiar. To understand how he might have arrived at his position, one must grasp certain facts, which, because of their specialized nature, may not be known even to the generally well-informed reader.

The census of 1897 revealed, in round figures, a population of 126 million in the Russian Empire, which, it must be remembered, at that time and for twenty years afterward included Poland. Of this figure, a little over five million (or over 4 per cent of the total) were Jews. The meaning of the Holocaust can be gauged concretely, by the way, from a simple consideration. While the population of Russia itself—despite three revolutions, two world wars, a bloody civil war, and the dismemberment of its empire—has doubled in seventy-five years, the Jewish population has been halved and now numbers less than three million in Russia and all its satellites combined —in other words around 1 per cent of the total.

In 1897, by far the greatest part of the Jewish population was concentrated into the Pale of Settlement, which constituted less than one twentieth of the territory of Russia. But even in this restricted area, the proportion of the Jewish to the non-Jewish population was only about 11 per cent. Outside it, Jews numbered less than half a percentage point of the population. On the other hand, the overwhelming majority of Jews (94 per cent) lived within the Pale, while only 6 per cent dwelt outside it. Even in well-known Jewish centers such as could be found in the governments of Vitebsk, Vilna, and Minsk, the Jewish concentration was no larger than 15 per cent, and in Warsaw itself less than 20 per cent of the population was Jewish.

Something should be said, perhaps, about the Pale of Settlement. Virtually everyone has heard of it, but few know precisely what it was or whence it came. The Pale was that portion of Russia in which Jews were permitted to reside, unlike other Russian subjects who could travel and live anywhere in Russia. Jews could leave the Pale only under conditions specified by law.

It had been established in 1791 when Byelorussian Jews who had come under Russian jurisdiction after the first partition of Poland in 1772 were forbidden to join merchant or artisan guilds other than those of Byelorussia. The limits of the Pale were modified from time to time. By 1794, it included, among others, the provinces of such administrative centers as Minsk, Bratzlav, Polotzk, and Kiev. To these were added in the next decade Vilna, Grodno, Courland, Astrakhan, and Caucasia. The situation was further complicated by the fact that Jews were forbidden to reside in certain places within the Pale itself, for example in the military ports of Sebastopol and Nikolaev, and in the city (as distinguished from the province) of Kiev. Exceptions were sometimes noted in the case of master workmen and contractors who worked for the military arm, but their apprentices might be excluded from the special "privileges" extended to themselves. And these arbitrary regulations were enforced by sudden, unannounced police raids and "searches" late at night designed to ferret out violators and, incidentally, to strike fear into everybody else. Immigrants to America later recalled such incidents with shudders when they recounted them to their children. Not only were Jews restricted in their rights of residence in large cities such as Kiev, they were also excluded from villages in the governments of Vitebsk and Mogilev, from crown lands everywhere, and from Cossack villages in the provinces of Chernigov and Poltava.

The dread attending violation of these ordinances can be appreciated only from reading some of the Yiddish memoirs of the period written by young men with an urge to travel and see the country but fearful at every instant of the consequences of getting caught breaking the rules.

Jews also continued to live in the provinces of Warsaw, Lomza, Lublin, Radom, and other

Polish places, but these were not included in the Pale, and until 1862, by an administrative ruling that still further hampered their freedom of movement, Jews in the Polish provinces were forbidden to reside in the Pale, and vice versa. The ostensible reason for these exclusions was to prevent economic exploitation of the population by the Jews, but it was generally recognized that this was a rationalization of powerful religious prejudices. By 1904, merchants belonging to the first guild might legally reside in Kiev, Sebastopol, and Nikolaev. Exceptions were also made in the case of persons possessing a secular higher education (which, however, was made very difficult to achieve through a strict quota system applied to Jews and systematic exclusions), for artisans and master-workmen, and finally for old soldiers in the Russian Army who had served for twenty-five years and more under the Draconic conscription laws of Nicholas I. Excluded from the tolerance of this dispensation were those veterans who had served for lesser periods under subsequent more liberal and lenient laws.

The number of Jewish artisans or handicraftsmen had been large since the middle of the nineteenth century, when the government, to encourage their development, had granted them the theoretical rights of residence anywhere in Russia. In Warsaw, the number of artisans was comparatively small (7½ per cent of the Jewish population), but in places like Grodno and Radom, it approached or exceeded 20 per cent.

Contrary to pernicious myths spread by their enemies and sometimes unfortunately believed by Jews themselves about their affinity for the less strenuous and supposedly parasitical role of middlemen in the economy, there were throughout eastern Europe, at the turn of the twentieth century, Jewish bakers, barbers, blacksmiths, bookbinders, butchers, cabinetmakers and joiners, capmakers, carpenters, coppersmiths, dressmakers, dyers, glaziers, locksmiths, piano tuners,

oven makers, bricklayers, painters, saddlers, harness makers, seamstresses, shoemakers, stocking makers, tailors, tanners, tobacco workers, watchmakers, weavers, and wigmakers. The distribution among these trades, as one might expect, was uneven. More than a third of the number was concentrated in tailoring and shoemaking, and sizable numbers could also be found in such vocations as dressmaking and cabinet construction (all of which helps to cast some light upon the development of the clothing, shoe, and furniture industries in the United States during the period of maximum immigration of Jews from eastern Europe).

It is certainly possible to oversimplify the picture of east European Jewry. There was a great variety of types there in addition to those we have usually heard about: *yeshiva* students, scholars, rabbis, innkeepers, peddlers, small entrepreneurs, some professional men, and large numbers of *Hasidim* who spent a deal of time singing, dancing, and occasionally imbibing at the "courts" of their favorite wonder-rabbis and *zaddikim* while their wives took care of providing material sustenance for their household by running a little store or having a stall in the marketplace. In addition to the craftsmen, there were even some Jewish farmers, though it must be admitted that their number was small, probably because ownership of land was one of the things forbidden to Jews, and at best they could hope to function only under the fiction of long-term leases from aristocratic, absentee landlords, who exacted from them a substantial share of the proceeds as rent in return for their "protection."

Jewish artisans acquired their skills in the old-fashioned way of apprenticeship, and their technical training was for long regarded as both backward and inadequate. Nevertheless, we are told on good authority that many of them soon proved themselves superior in practice, and in the large cities, where in the twentieth century there was an increasing demand for articles of better workmanship, the Jews were able to provide the best tailors, shoemakers, joiners, watchmakers, and so on. These hand-workers were hardly well paid for their labors. Competition was keen and conditions of credit unfavorable, so that the average income of tailors in Poland, for example, during the first decade of the twentieth century was from 250 to 300 rubles a year (a ruble being worth at that time about half a dollar); that of Jewish shoemakers ranged from 150 to 250 rubles a year; and seamstresses earned still less (100 rubles annually). Lacemakers, for whose delicate and demanding work there was only a short, seasonal demand, earned no more than an average of 45 rubles a year.

Conditions were somewhat more prosperous in southern Russia, where it is said that some Jewish artisans were able to earn as much as 1,000 rubles a year. But it is hardly surprising to learn that, in the Pale, the incomes were often not sufficient to support the families of artisans, and numbers of them could hardly eke out a bare living with their best efforts and were compelled occasionally to subsist on the charitable aid of their brethren. Artisans allowed to live outside the Pale had to do so on temporary permits that could be withdrawn if for any reason they left or changed their callings. In any case, they still depended on their native communities and were often subjected to harassment and extortion by the local authorities of these places, which made it impossible for any large number of them to take advantage of any relaxation in official policy toward the Jews. Even under the liberal reign of Alexander II, fewer than seven hundred artisans managed to extricate themselves from the Pale and to establish workshops in the governments of Saint Petersburg, Smolensk, Pskov, Orel, Kursk, Voronezh, Saratov, and Moscow. The punitive May Laws of 1882

forced many of them to abandon their new homes.

It was in eastern Europe that Jews developed the habit, tradition, and indeed instinct for mutual aid that was later to elicit the admiration of the world. Mark Twain in his well-known essay "Concerning the Jews" set down certain conclusions based upon his observation during the height of the great immigrant period:

The Jew is not a burden on the charities of the state nor of the city; these could cease from their functions without affecting him. When he is well enough, he works; when he is incapacitated, his own people take care of him. And not in a poor or stingy way, but with a fine and large benevolence. His race is entitled to be called the most benevolent of all the races of men. . . . The charitable institutions of the Jews are supported by Jewish money, and amply. The Jews make no noise about it; it is done quietly; they do not nag and pester and harass us for contributions; they give us peace, and set us an example—an example which we have not found ourselves able to follow.

All accounts agree that mutual aid was one of the most important expressions of the religious spirit in eastern Europe. Unfortunately, the demand on the generosity of the Jews was unlimited, while the resources available to them were only too limited. In 1898, the Passover charities in 1,200 Russian towns reported that more than 132,000 Jews had applied for relief. Statistics indicate that the number of paupers in the most sizable centers of Jewish population approached 20 per cent. The figures are smaller, though still large, in places like Warsaw; they are largest in Grodno, Lublin, and Vilna. Yet it was estimated that the number of the destitute reported was far below the actual cases, since the tradition of the community was quite "reticent" with respect to applying for help even when it was necessary. Admission of need was considered shameful and a disgrace by most people there. Immigrants like Morris Raphael Cohen later recalled with pride parents and grandparents who were too self-conscious to ask for relief even when their families had no bread to eat. It was reported that there were some imaginative people in the Pale who ostentatiously walked about the streets sporting toothpicks in their mouths to create the impression that they had just eaten when in reality it was difficult for them to recall when they had last had a square meal. Given this sort of psychology, it is possible to assume that the number of the poor actually reported might have been an understatement.

In the Pale alone, there were more than fifty societies to help brides who were poor. Their income was derived from collections made every Friday, since Jews could be expected to be more generous than they could afford on the eve of their Sabbath. There were over five hundred societies of a generally charitable kind. Medical committees in small towns arranged with the local physician for free treatment of the poor, and they occasionally sent patients to health resorts or cities where more advanced types of treatment were available. More important, perhaps, members of these committees sometimes *took turns in nursing the sick*. There were more than a hundred houses of shelter for the transient poor. Benevolent associations made loan-funds available without charging interest to help artisans and small traders carry on their business independently. Many of these associations were not even incorporated and were managed by one or several trustees. An exception to the rule was the Grodno benevolent association, which was incorporated with a capital stock of 7,000 rubles in the year 1900. There was a loan-bank in Warsaw, which made advances of small amounts without charging any interest, although it did take minimal pledges as security. In 1901 alone, this large-scale charitable enterprise accommodated more than 6,600 people and its loans aggregated over 76,000 rubles.

In America the image of the philanthropist is the rather cynical one of a robber baron in his old age endowing a museum, a library, or a college. And it is this image that inspired Irving Babbitt to write: "What a man owes to society in the final analysis is not his philanthropy but a good example." That is true. The example of conduct is our most important social contribution, but one must hardly forget that philanthropy, as Mark Twain was so keenly aware, is itself a potent example, and it is one upon which Jewish tradition lays great stress. From this point of view, a remark made by the translator of one of the novels of Mendele Mocher Seforim is entirely beside the point. He is disgusted by the spectacle of all the bustling charitable activities carried on among the east European Jews and writes: "Among the pauperized Jews, [philanthropic] societies flourished like weeds on a dung-heap. There were burial societies, welfare societies, *kashruth* societies, sickness societies. . . . These societies were supported by the miserable kopecks scraped together from the poor. . . ."

That is the no-nonsense statement of an *esprit fort*. It is, however, not mere cant or sentimentality to insist that donations that are not made out of a superfluity of goods but represent a true sacrifice are ennobling to the giver, or that a society in which giving till it hurt was the prevailing custom was improved by it. This is not to say that there were no connivers, crooks, chiselers, exploiters, and even gangsters among the Jews of eastern Europe who took advantage of this tradition. The pages of satirists like Linetski and Mendele and even of romantics like Sholem Asch are there to vouch for their existence. But it is significant that thirty years after writing *Dos Kleine mentschele* (which is a bitter exposure of the parasitical excrescences upon Jewish communal life), its author Mendele is quoted by Lucy Dawidowicz with some second thoughts about the danger of confusing the parasite with the host upon which it preys. To restore balance to the impression created by some of his satires, Mendele wrote at the turn of the century:

> The life of the congregation of Israel, though it appears outwardly ugly, is nevertheless inwardly beautiful. A powerful spirit dwells in Jewish life, a divine spirit which like a gusting wind raises waves to cleanse them of filth and decay. Beneath the refuse of the cheder, the yeshivahs and the prayer houses, the flame of Torah glows, casting light and warmth among the whole people. All our children, poor and rich, small and great, have mastered Hebrew letters and are immersed in study. Such a life we say is right, and it is fitting to record it for generations to come.

How the general ethos was reflected in everyday life can be gleaned from a little anecdote in Maurice Hindus's memoir, *Green Worlds*. His father was an ordinary, representative man in every respect, but what distinguished him from his peasant neighbors in the village where he lived was his feeling of belonging to the larger Jewish community in the city to which he went with his family for the important holidays and being bound by its traditions as he interpreted them:

> Whenever a beggar stopped at our house, father saw to it that he got the best food we had, better than we ate. If mother had eggs or butter that she was saving for the bazaar, he would ask her to share them with the beggar. To him a beggar was the ward of God, and he would not offend God by withholding from his ward anything he might have in the house. Naturally I came to regard a beggar as the most privileged person in the world. Merely by being what he was he could command in our house the best of food and shelter. Only the constable or some other uniformed official might be similarly pampered by mother and father, and not out of respect or reverence, like a beggar, but out of fear or abasement. Once

mother set before a passing constable a jar of honey which she had received as a gift from a neighbor. Honey was so precious a delicacy that a thin spread on a thick slice of bread brought shouts of glee from old and young in the family. The constable dipped endless slices of bread into the jar, and after he had eaten all the honey he wiped clean with his fingers the sides of the vessel. When he was gone there was grumbling and weeping in the house, and mother pronounced on him a formidable curse. Yet, had it been a beggar who had made away with the whole jar of honey, she would have scolded us for grumbling and weeping. I envied beggars more than I did the merchants, the lumbermen and the other well-to-do people who passed through our villages, and I resolved that when I grew up I would be a beggar.

The anecdote would be more suspect than it is were it not confirmed in essential respects by independent testimony from other quarters. Mordecai Spector's charming Yiddish story "A Meal for the Poor" deals in humorous fashion with the real power exercised by the *batlanim* and *bettlers* (beggars) in an east European community. A Jew, according to a widely quoted and authoritative traditional definition there, is one who "sorrows" and feels compassion for every form of life, and to have a good "Jewish heart," when judged by such a criterion of universal kindness and sympathy, was a common aspiration. It may, in fact, be this quality that has given to its culture a tinge, a soupçon of sentimentality that on occasion has been critically remarked on by those not basically attuned to it, including some who are Jews themselves.

With insignificant exceptions, however, those who emerged out of the matrix of that culture and studied it long and reflected deeply upon the fruits of the spirit which it produced, even when their own outlook departed far from it and they themselves became broadly secular, intellectually liberated and "Western" in their outlook, have pronounced weighty verdicts in its favor. So we find the historian Dubnow noting with unashamed sentiment (which is something very different from lachrymose sentimentality) that

> Jewish history possesses the student with the conviction that Jewry at all times . . . was preeminently a spiritual nation, and a spiritual nation it continues to be in our days, too. . . . Judaism, which has accomplished great things for humanity in the past, has not yet played out its part, and, therefore, may not perish. In short, the Jewish people lives because it contains a living soul which refuses to separate from its integument, and cannot be forced out of it by heavy trials and misfortunes, such as would unfailingly inflict mortal injury upon less sturdy organisms.

There is something cumulatively impressive about the tributes paid to the east European way of life by people who knew it from experience, despite the fact that they later moved away from its guiding assumptions in the direction of philosophic rationalism and skepticism. Morris Raphael Cohen tells us that the years he spent with his grandfather in Neshwies laid the foundations not only of his later intellectual development but of his moral life as well. Looking back, more than half a century later, he thought that the Jewish life in that town proved that people find happiness when they don't strain too hard to do so. Nothing was important there but the dictates of religion, which were known to all. It was a life lacking in the civilized amenities to which he later became accustomed, but he found there a sustaining peace of mind, spiritual security, and an admirable superiority to those who were more materialistically inclined. "Renunciation led to fulfillment," he writes. He learned there the wisdom of living frugally (which is not to say in a miserly fashion) by choice rather than of necessity and to maintain an attitude of detachment from luxuries of which fate might deprive him arbitrarily at any moment.

Mary Antin, who was starry-eyed about "The Promised Land" (America) and denigrated almost everything she experienced in the first thirteen years of her life in the Russian Pale, nevertheless waxed quite poetic on the subject of the unsuspected spiritual riches that had fallen to her lot in being born in Polotzk:

> When I came to lie on my mother's breast, she sang me lullabies on lofty themes. I heard the names of Rebecca, Rachel, and Leah as early as the names of father, mother and nurse. My baby soul was enthralled by sad and noble cadences, as my mother sang of my ancient home in Palestine, or mourned over the desolation of Zion. With the first rattle that was placed in my hand a prayer was pronounced over me, a petition that a pious man might take me to wife, and a messiah be among my sons. . . . I was fed on dreams, instructed by means of prophecies, trained to hear and see mystical things that callous senses could not perceive. I was taught to call myself a princess, in memory of my forefathers who had ruled a nation. Though I went in the disguise of an outcast, I felt a halo resting on my brow. Set upon by brutal enemies, unjustly hated, annihilated a hundred times, I yet arose and held my head high, sure that I should find my kingdom in the end, although I had lost my way in exile; for He who had brought my ancestors safe through a thousand perils was guiding my feet as well. God needed me as I needed Him, for we two together had a work to do, according to an ancient covenant between Him and my forefathers.

These tributes were all paid before the Holocaust and are therefore exempt from any doubt about whether they originated in pious deference to the prudent maxim: *"De mortuis nil nisi bonum"* (of the departed, let us say nothing that is not good). The east European Jew was reminded daily by the Psalmist, whose words he recited, that though man-in-himself was less than nothing and had no claim upon divine bounty, his creator was mindful of him and had given him dominion over the animal creation and made him but little lower than the angels. The moral of such a world-outlook could not but rub off on the conduct of life. Though the Jew himself was sometimes treated like a captive animal, he was reminded continually of the divine assurance that he was not only a man but a man singled out for special distinction. Life in the *shtetl* could be described as having some analogies to life on the sides of a dozing volcano, which intermittently erupted. Yet could not the situation of man himself be described in similar terms? When the volcano of human passions was silent for a decade or several decades, the Jew attained a feeling of safety, comfort, and forgetfulness of what it was like under more threatening conditions. In the interstices of what Stephen Dedalus in *Ulysses* calls the nightmare of history, the Jew in eastern Europe was able to construct for himself out of his poverty-stricken materials a way of life and an image of human worth and dignity comparable to any that he or other men had fashioned. That was probably as true on the eve of his destruction as it had ever been, and it is a feat that invites us to inquire more precisely how it was accomplished.

Krakow Street

Market Entrance

Courtyard in Warsaw

Vegetable Market

Jewish Market, Warsaw

Rowne Porter

At the Pump

Weary Man

Old Clothes Market

To the Market

Fish Market

Patient Shopkeeper

Glazier, Lublin

Bake Oven

Gravestone Carver

Cemetery, Prague

Vilna Street

Rhythms
of Religious
Existence

WHAT WAS THE SECRET of the Jew's feeling of security in insecurity that prompted a son of the *shtetl,* Abraham Joshua Heschel, to describe it in an eloquent threnody after its disappearance in the following manner?

There, in Eastern Europe, the Jewish people came into its own. It did not live like a guest in somebody else's house, who must constantly keep in mind the ways and customs of the host. There Jews lived without reservation and without disguise, outside their homes no less than within them. When they used the phrase "the world asks" in their commentaries on the Talmud, they did not refer to a problem raised by Aristotle or Averroës. Their fellow students of Torah were to them the "world."

Is this ecstatic description unrealistic? Certainly it is unrealistic! If one were inclined to make picayune puns, nothing would be easier than to fasten on such exaggerations as in the statement "There the Jews lived *without reservation...*" and to point out that, if one thing is certain, it is that the Jews in eastern Europe lived *within a reservation,* like the aborigines in this country, a vast ghetto fenced off and separated from the rest of mankind. That is surely true, and yet is there not some higher truth in Heschel's heightened poetic vision? The great attraction of the heartfelt faith that filled the Jewish communities of eastern Europe over many generations, from the point of view of the modern caught in the chaotic contemporary wasteland, is the meaningful shape and form that it gave to everyday existence. Every act of life, no matter how humble, was accorded recognition, from the moment of awakening, which was marked by the pouring of "fingernail water" over the hands and the saying of the prayer *modi ani* (the first one that every Jewish child learned) to the saying of *Kriath Shema* before going to sleep at night. A spiritual leader as distinguished as the Vilna Gaon, commenting on the custom of rinsing of one's mouth with water in the morning, attributes it to the necessity of *cleansing one's mouth for prayer.*

Ahad Ha'am, in his essay entitled "Ancestor Worship," observes that in an age of faith,

Just as medical science is not ashamed to treat of the hidden organs of the human body, so the Torah could not leave untouched any jot or tittle of the minutiae of life, be they ever so repulsive. ...The Jew of those days felt his life and his individuality only so long as he was surrounded by an atmosphere of Torah. Let him leave that atmosphere for a moment, and it was as though he had suddenly entered a strange world.... The Jews needed "laws and ritual ordinances," fixed immutably and beyond question, possessed of an authority backed by force, and capable of giving a definite religious form to the whole content of life, down to the smallest detail.

From this point of view, it is possible to say that the concerns of Deuteronomy, Chapter 23, verses 13–15, which seem so absurd to a philosopher like Shestov, are not at all absurd. The form that Hebrew humanism took was the feeling that nothing human was so alien or noisome as to make it unworthy of notice and indeed sanctification. To give only one striking instance of the minute scrutiny and regulation lavished upon every aspect of life, if a man on the eve of the Sabbath included among his preparations the paring of his fingernails, there were precise instructions in the Talmud about the order of the fingers from which he must cut them!

The ceremonial accompaniments of the most prosaic of daily duties gave the average man a feeling of accomplishment that eventually produced a conviction of purposefulness of life. Sholom Aleichem's dairyman Tevya stops his horse and wagon in the middle of a wood where his profitless search for a living has brought him and where there is no eye but God's to see him, because the time has come to say his afternoon prayers. And there is no sense of incongruity in his daring to address the Lord with an intimate familiarity equal to that achieved by any of the Hasidic masters celebrated by Martin Buber. The sly satiric thrusts of the author at his char-

acter are somehow compatible with the kindliness of the sentiment he inspires.

Even the Jewish convict in Siberia whom Dostoevski encounters in *The House of the Dead* performs his devotions as scrupulously and enthusiastically as Tevya does, and the other prisoners (including the protagonist, who can hardly be suspected of philo-Semitism) watch with fascination as he dares to proclaim his own religious identity before them.

The great pillars that structured the daily life were the morning, afternoon, and evening prayers, which, if at all possible, would be said in *shul,* for though individual prayer was permitted it was not encouraged and there was special merit in joining one's prayer with that of a congregation. So delicious did some find this social experience that they sought every pretext to visit the synagogue more often than tradition required. No business, duty, or distraction was permitted to interfere with the saying of prayers. Whatever a man might be doing, in company or alone, on a train or in an office, he felt compelled by habit, if by no loftier motive, when the proper time came, to discharge his elementary obligation to the divine world with his daily prayers.

Far behind the three prayers in importance came the three meals that sustained the Jew's physical existence. These concessions to appetite were carefully hedged about with *berakhas* (blessings) and saying of grace, which acted as continual reminders of human dependence on the divine. The pious tended to be rather abstemious in their indulgences upon principle. The attention of the human mind was directed away from the senses. Franz Kafka's haunting association of spirituality with self-denial (which appears in its most concentrated form in his story "The Hunger Artist" but can be found in other works of his, including his best-known one, "Metamorphosis"), although it is no doubt applicable to ascetic religions in general, could have been inspired by a meditation on the life-style of the old-fashioned east European Jew in particular. Kafka's personal view, to be sure, is much more modern and must not be confused with that of his compulsively abstinent charac-ters. "It is better to bite Life," he once wrote in a letter to Oskar Pollak, "than to bite one's tongue." His characters, however, are lacking in both teeth and appetite. As for the east European Jews, they could hardly have "bitten life" even if they had been minded to do so, and in the final analysis they probably didn't even wish to.

Just as the day was divided and structured by its three great periods of prayer, so the week found its center in the Sabbath and the year its form in a series of holidays that included the twelve monthly blessings of the New Moon, since the Jewish calendar is a lunar one. The importance of the Sabbath in the scheme of things may be gauged from the fact that the sanctity of the holiest fast-day of the year, *Yom Kippur,* is reckoned to be no more than that of a double Sabbath. But unlike *Yom Kippur,* with its disciplinary penance, contrition, and atone-ment, the Sabbath is associated in the minds of the smallest and the most exalted with visions of plenty.

"The one glimmer of light in our lives was the Sabbath," writes an immigrant who was not in the least Orthodox. "With irrepressible long-ing we waited for its arrival, and with over-whelming sorrow we mourned its departure. On the Sabbath we were sure of getting a slice of white bread at each meal and sugar for our tea and meat at least during one meal. The white bread was such a luxury now that we often ate it with black bread as we did the slice of egg with which mother now and then surprised and delighted us."

The Sabbath drew into its orbit the day that preceded it, for preparations of cooking and cleaning had to begin early on Friday. Jewish culinary art is not celebrated, yet the most stub-born rationalists confess to feeling their mouths water as they remember the taste or savor of *cholent* (a baked dish of meat and potatoes) on Saturday afternoons, *chalah* (white bread), *tzimis* (a dish combining cooked carrots and turnips), chicken soup, and fish prepared in a distinctive and appetizing way. Women played an impor-tant ancillary role on the Sabbath, ushering it in with the lighting of candles, covering their faces with their hands, closing their eyes, and murmuring two prayers while doing so: one in Hebrew, which is the same as that pronounced by every other daughter of Israel, and the other, on behalf of their loved ones, in the homelier language Yiddish, which they understood.

The Sabbath is conceived of poetically in the liturgy as a Queen and a Bride, and it is ushered out as ceremoniously with the recitation of the *havdala* prayer and the lighting of a long braided wax candle by the father on Saturday evening as it had been ushered in by the mother on Friday afternoon. *Kiddush,* or a benediction over a cup of wine, accompanies the return of the man from evening prayers in the synagogue on each of these occasions. Such sacraments, faith-fully performed by those who are even slightly gifted musically and possess some aesthetic sense of the possibilities of creating beauty in ritual, are colorful and imaginatively impressive enough to make many of those who either participated in or witnessed them in their original settings cherish their memories for a lifetime.

There was also, however, some anxiety con-nected with the day. Heeding all the restrictions upon one's activity on the day of rest was not easy. Some must have been especially hard to live with. Cooking was forbidden; tearing paper was forbidden; striking a light was forbidden; smoking was not permitted; carrying anything (even so light a thing as a handkerchief, or keys in one's pocket, or one's prayer book and *tallith* on the way to *shul*) was not permitted. The pious tied their handkerchiefs around their wrists (which was permitted), and if a group of houses that included the synagogue was "fenced around" with a cord or wire on the Sabbath, each householder might then treat the enclosed area as if it were his own home (which meant he could carry his prayer book), according to an accepted interpretation of rabbinical law. Carrying over the Old World Sabbath to America proved almost impossible for many immigrants, and those who coped with the difficulties were so proud of their feat that to this day one can read Hebrew inscriptions on the tombstones in immigrant cemeteries indicating that an individual's claim to fame was that "all of his days" he had been a faithful "guardian of the Sabbath." Well might he preen himself upon such a distinction, for in the economy of the New World such observance often entailed some sacrifices that the impecunious believer could ill afford.

PASSOVER

Strictly speaking, an account of the Jewish holidays should begin with the celebration of the lunar New Year, which generally occurs toward the end of September, and formal treatises on the subject begin at that point. If this were done, the holiday of Passover, which is a spring holiday, would wind up somewhere near the end of the procession. Yet, since it is the most universally beloved and appreciated of the festivals, a case can be made for beginning with it. A fable told by women in the old country concerned a Gentile who had become converted to the Jewish faith just before Passover, and when that bright festivity rolled around, he thought that he had struck a very good bargain

in his new religion. But later on, in the summer, when he had to join his fellow Jews in their Black Fast of *Tisha b'Ab* (the ninth day of the lunar month of *Ab,* which commemorates the destruction of the ancient Temple) and still more so during the Days of Awe, which reach from *Rosh Hashana* (New Year's) to the fast of *Yom Kippur,* the Jewish world-outlook seemed to the new convert to take on an altogether more somber coloration, and he was not at all sure any longer about the wisdom of the choice he had made. The women told the tale with a little laugh and a sense of satisfaction, for was it not a perfect parable about the trials as well as the joys associated with being a Jew? Only one who was "dyed in the wool" realized that he must accept and glory in the pains as well as the pleasures of his condition.

Passover was definitely a pleasure, but it was hard work, too, especially for the women, for there were exotic foods to be prepared and it was the time of the general spring cleaning. Everything had to be scrubbed until it shone, even the nooks and crannies where nobody ever looked. Special dishes and cutlery that were used only during this week of the year had to be taken down, and the plates, knives, and spoons regularly used had to be packed and stored in the attic. Fresh curtains were put up, and everyone in the house had to be outfitted with new clothes. Shmarya Levin, in his memoirs, quite rightly refers to Passover as "the greatest and most splendid of the festivals," and he is representative of a great number of east Europeans who have shared their recollections with the public when he adds that "nothing, in the memories of my childhood years, shines so clearly and so lovingly as this evening of Passover."

Many of the Jewish holidays give an important place to the children in the celebrations, but none more so than Passover. A boy must be a clod if his fancy is not taken the night before as he accompanies his father on the ritual search for the last traces of *hametz* (or leaven), which must be removed from the house. In the east European town, this meant that one must come prepared with a lighted candle in one hand and a goose feather and wooden spoon in the other. A man can use help for all of this paraphernalia and a boy is called upon to lend a hand. The search is not a serious one, of course, since the mother has placed the bread crumbs in locations well known beforehand to the father, who is "looking for" them, but that hardly keeps it from being an exciting adventure for a small boy. Next morning, the father lights a fire in the yard back of the house and burns every trace of leaven he has gathered the night before, along with the feather and spoon that he used in gathering it. The household can now be considered ritually pure.

When the *seder* is performed in an orderly fashion, and each of its fifteen separate steps is scrupulously carried out, it becomes a ceremony the fullness of which may dwarf the feast that is at its center. Here, as elsewhere, the observant in the *shtetl* put the physical in its subordinate place by the magnificence of the literary and musical setting with which they surrounded it. The youngest child asks the famous "four questions" to which the company responds with an extensive recitative about the history of the ancient Jews in Egypt, their sufferings, and their miraculous liberation from bondage under the benign leadership of Moses.

After the meal, traditionally introduced by hard-boiled eggs dipped in salt water, there follow a melodious grace, Psalms, and as an epilogue to the ceremony (which includes, by the way, four sacramental cups of wine for each guest, not counting the unquaffed cup set for the prophet Elijah), a series of rollicking songs, the charm of which can hardly be reproduced for those who have not been introduced to them in earliest childhood. A child waited through the whole year with the keenest anticipation of these magical evenings and sang his heart out with joy while feeling the ceremony draw inexorably to an end. The delight was indissoluble from the sadness over the passage of time, over what one would later learn to call the mutability of things, and over the transitoriness of life's loveliest moments. It was like one's first experience of reading a fascinating book and trying to slow the inevitable moment when the last page would be reached.

Certain customs centered upon the eating of the *aphikoman*, which is the twelfth step in the procedure of the *seder*. This is the *matzo* that was "hidden" at the beginning of the service by the master of the house until the conclusion of the meal. While grownups wink at their transgression, some of the children abscond with the consecrated *matzo* and, at the proper point at which it becomes indispensable for the continuation of the ceremony, it must be *ransomed* from them, which makes them feel both accomplished and naughty. The curious word *aphikoman* has been traced to the Greek word επικωμοι or dessert, and it represents the paschal lamb, which was traditionally the last thing to be eaten during the meal in antiquity, so that its taste might linger longest in the mouth. It was believed by some of the younger members of the household that if one could resist the temptation to devour the precious mouthful of *aphikoman* immediately and save part of it, it would bring its possessor good luck throughout the remainder of the year. Sometimes, such a person would display at the *seder* a piece of the *aphikoman* of the preceding year, and its crumbling residue might occasionally be found by an east European Jewish tailor in the pocket of a garment that had been given to him to be pressed or cleaned.

Yet, this brilliant festival, despite all its innocent pleasures, was not without its shadows of trepidation, if not for the children then for their elders, who had longer memories and had read some history. For the latter were aware that the Passover *seder* had entered the Christian story as The Last Supper and that perhaps because of this sinister association, ever since the Middle Ages and particularly in the lands of eastern Europe, Jews were repeatedly accused of murdering Christian children and using their blood in the preparation of *matzos*. It hardly mattered that a series of Popes had labeled the accusation a libel or that a modern scholar of Semitology, Ernest Renan, had declared it a baseless fabrication. The important thing was that *muzhiks* on a rampage still believed it and were capable of using it as a rationalization to disguise their own impulses to plunder and kill. So pregnant with suggestion of this kind was the atmosphere of eastern Europe that as late as 1911 the Russian government countenanced the trial of Mendel Beiliss in the city of Kiev on a charge of ritual murder. The trial was reported throughout the world, and though Beiliss was acquitted by the jury, the very fact that the charge could be brought and debated in the twentieth century is eloquent testimony to the situation of the Jews of eastern Europe. The Beiliss case, through the interest of the immigrants, entered into the American Jewish tradition, which explains the appearance in the last decade of two literary works dealing with it: Maurice Samuel's history, *Blood Accusation,* and Bernard Malamud's prize-winning novel, *The Fixer.*

OTHER HOLIDAYS

It has been remarked of the Jews in eastern Europe that though they were poor in every other respect (they were certainly the original "Jews without money"), they were extraordinarily rich in the number of festivals they celebrated. These were some holidays observed by the Jews in the Old World that are hardly known even by name to their descendants here. The customs of other holidays that are better known to us differed widely in the Old World from those familiar to us. An example of one of the lesser-known holidays is what has been called the New Year of the Trees, or in (Hebrew) *Chamishe Osor Be-Shebat,* which simply means the fifteenth day of the lunar month of *shebat,* when the trees, not of eastern Europe but of the Holy Land, experience their resurrection in the spring. The teacher in the *heder* carefully explained to the children that in the Holy Land there is no real winter or cold or snow, and the fruit trees bloom early with figs and dates, locust, oranges, and pomegranates, which are unknown in colder climes. He urged them all to bring plenty of fruit to the *heder* that day to celebrate, and if they found it difficult to get such exotic fruit as pomegranates and oranges, they did manage to bring figs and dates.

The holiday of *Lag b'Omer* is celebrated on the thirty-third day of "the Omer," that is, the seven-week period between Passover and Pentecost. It marks the abatement of the plague among the disciples of Rabbi Akiba in the time of Bar Kochba, who for three years led the last great revolt of the Jews against Rome, which broke out in the year 132 of the Christian era. The boys brought hard-boiled, colored eggs to *heder,* that day. The eggs acquired their colors from being boiled together with onion leeks, nettle leaves, and other plants. With these eggs they played a game that they had learned from the Gentile boys who played it at Easter. It consisted of each of the contestants holding his egg at the broad end and tapping the narrow end against that of his opponent until the more fragile of the two shells cracked. At the end of the game, the boy who had the egg with the hardest shell and was unvanquished became the owner of all the eggs that had broken.

On *Tisha b'Ab,* to commemorate the fall of the Temple, a youngster would be astonished to watch his elders swallowing horrible mouthfuls of rolls dipped in ashes! In the synagogue that day everyone sat in his stockinged feet, exactly as one did in the house of a mourner. The lamps were left unlighted after night fell. Following the evening prayer, the congregation sat on the floor, and the reading of the Book of Lamentations began. The combination of darkness, lugubrious melody, and the sound of universal weeping, softly from the men's section and more audibly from the women's section (for the sexes were, of course, severely separated from each other during religious services), chilled the soul of every listener and terrified the young.

On *Purim,* if the town boasted of any theatrical talent at all, a miracle play was performed, based on the events narrated in the Scroll of Esther. Preparations for this great event might take up the better part of a month, since the actors were apprenticed to various trades, and the "director" himself might be a tailor by day. Sympathetic parts such as those of Mordecai, Queen Esther, and King Ahasuerus were sought after, but no one wanted the villainous part of Haman except the dramatically ambitious, to whom it presented a challenge. When Haman appeared on stage, a thrill of fear ran through the audience ready to respond primitively to the momentary mask adopted by the player and to forget that underneath it was no furious enemy of the Jews but one of their own neighbors.

The *sukkah* on the festival of *Sukkoth* was a ramshackle booth improvised out of anything one could get hold of: thin planks, old doors, windows, and so on. It was a small house without a roof, and to cover it on top, branches of fir were used. The rituals of this holiday were colorful, involving the *lulab,* or slender palm, and the *ethrog,* or citron, both brought from Palestine a thousand miles away, and willows gathered from the fields around.

On *Simhath Torah,* or the day of the Rejoicing of the Law, when the reading of the last chapter of the Pentateuch is concluded, pious Jews dance ecstatically with the Scroll of the Law, as with a bride in their arms. The Torah is crowned with silver and decked out in velvet and silks, and it is no light burden. It is interesting that in contemporary Russia, the one Jewish holiday that has gained most in popularity as an expression of national solidarity and in defiance of the determined antireligious propaganda of the regime is *Simhath Torah,* when for years Jewish youth by thousands have not only filled the few synagogues remaining but the streets around.

In connection with *Rosh Hashana,* there were customs among east European Jews that have virtually disappeared from the memory of their descendants. One of the most discussed was the psychologically fascinating ritual known as *tashlik,* when the community went down to the river and symbolically "shook off" into it the sins of the past year. The ceremony involved shaking the lower part of one's coat over the water, though many went further than this by also turning their pockets inside out. No doubt there were many who, like the flirtatious couple in an amusing story by I. B. Singer, merely went through the motions and took the meaning of it with more than one grain of salt. But there were others (*not* adolescents in the throes of young love) who accepted it all more literally, were amenable to suggestion, and have testified to the feeling of relief and lightness that they experienced afterward.

Yom Kippur itself, when the Heavenly tribunal weighed each man's soul in the balance and sealed sentences of life and death, prosperity or the reverse, for the coming year, was an awe-inspiring day indeed in Jewish eastern Europe, the very pinnacle of its moral and religious fervor. Each male congregant that day was attired in a special white robe or *kittel;* he wore no shoes in the synagogue but was either in his slippers or his stockinged feet. The melodies were especially piercing, and one of them, the *Kol Nidre,* is probably the single best-known Jewish air. There were portions of the service when not merely the cantor but all men were expected to prostrate themselves in humility before the Almighty. On the windowsills of the synagogue, soul-lights brought by individual worshipers burned all through the night and the following day. There were some men that day who chose to submit themselves to *malkoth,* or stripes, performed on their bare backs on the floor of the synagogue by some pious mendicant or attendant whom they paid for his services. The hearts of sensitive children were strongly gripped with strange emotions as they witnessed grown men voluntarily undergoing a shameful and painful form of punishment that they them-

selves knew from experience in the *heder.* Some zealots and enthusiasts were determined to remain standing at their prayers throughout the whole twenty-four-hour period, in which no bite of food or drop of water was suffered to pass the lips, and the strength of their sheer determination helped them to triumph over the feebleness of the flesh. These were mostly men, but it was not unknown for women too, despite any frailty, to vie with them in heroic endurance.

There was also the touching custom, just before *Yom Kippur* began, of begging for forgiveness and reconciliation from those with whom one had quarreled during the year or whom one had, wittingly or unwittingly, hurt or wronged in some way, since tradition tells that God may forgive the transgressions of men against Himself on this day if He pleases but is powerless to forgive those of men against each other. That must be done by men themselves. Parents were not too proud to humble themselves before children on such an occasion and vice versa. From all accounts, when pietism was at its peak, all this was more than just a formality.

Home from Synagogue, Lithuania

Bialystok Beth Hamidrash

Galician Rabbi

Kiddush

Shtetl *Discussion*

Yeshiva Student

Tashlik

To the Synagogue

Beth Hamidrash, *Lublin*

Wooden Synagogue, North of Lublin

Galician Student

Hasidim, *Lwow*

Galician with Streimel

Polish Youth

Man of Letters

Sketches, Hasidim

Tarnopol Synagogue

The Load

Shoemaker

Cloth Merchant

Wood Turner

Outside Kaunas, Lithuania

Minstrels

Knife Grinder

Water Carrier

Wienianawa, Lublin

Lyuboml

Zloczow

Muddy Stream, Zloczow

Zloczow Washday

AT THE PUMP

At the Pump near Cluj, Romania

Krakow Market

Lublin Outskirts

Street Fiddler

Mitzvah *Tanz*

Ghetto Nests, Chelm

Tarnopol

Laundry

The Stream in Stryj

Secondhand Shop

Negative
Features

SUPERSTITION IS the wrong side of the medal of religion. One of the superstitions that attached itself to the intensity of the experience of *Yom Kippur* concerned the soul-candles that burned not only in the synagogue but in the home as well. These memorialized the dead, but candles were also lighted for the souls of the living, and if a candle burned down to the socket it was considered a good omen, but if it did not then the family was certain to be visited by death during the coming year.

In one family, a harrowing ghost story was told about a *Yom Kippur* eve soon after the patriarch and matriarch who told the story were married. The young couple retired for the night after returning from the synagogue, and the young husband had a dream in which he thought he saw his own father in earnest conversation with his bride's father, who had died some years before. The latter was saying: "What can a father do? I've been trying to awaken him to tell him that his soul-candle is going out, but he goes on sleeping!" At that moment, the young man awakened with a start and noticed that the candle was indeed flickering very low and seemed about to go out, but as he got up and sat beside it for a while the flame revived and burned full and bright again, so he decided to go back to bed. He had hardly gone to sleep when he was awakened by the same dream, and once again was startled to see that his soul-candle seemed about to go out. So without disturbing his sleeping wife, he arose and sat beside it until it burned bright again. He had hardly gone to sleep again, however, when his "night-visitors" returned a third time and scolded him with angry voices, calling him by his name: "Moses, what is the matter with you? Didn't we tell you before to get up? Your light is going out!" When he awoke this time and saw that it was indeed so, he decided at last to awaken his wife and tell her about his dreams, and the two of them sat up together beside the candle and did not go back to sleep for the rest of the night, and the light did not go out when the morning came. That was all there was to the tale, but the grandchildren listening to their grandparents telling it shivered with apprehension and the absolute certainty that, had the timely warning not been given by the supernatural emissary, the soul-candle would surely have been extinguished, and death would have entered that house without fail and taken away the very ancestor who was here before them today.

The authentic flavor of the old Jewish life in the *shtetl,* when it is successfully recaptured, as in Ansky's perennially popular play, *The Dybbuk,* or in the stories of I. B. Singer, is inseparable from such phenomena as demons, spirits, ghosts, and the possessed. The girl in the small town who would go to the cemetery in order to invite her departed relatives to be present at her wedding knew nothing about modern sophistications or research into extrasensory perception. She was entirely wholehearted, naive, and sincere, because the boundaries between the visible and invisible worlds, which seem so clear and definite to us, were in her mind blurred, vague, or nonexistent. Her active imagination had been thickly sown with old wives' tales, all of which had long traditions behind them. A seventeenth-century writer who was observant and detached noted curiously that "there is no country in which the Jews occupy themselves so much with mystic fantasies, devilism, talismans, and the invocation of spirits as in Poland."

The same complaint is voiced two centuries later by Joel Linetski in his autobiographical novel *Dos Poylische yingl (The Polish Lad).* In this satire, which has at times an almost Juvenalian ferocity, he tells us of the mixture of sacred and profane in the Jewish small-town life familiar to him, which started in the very cradle in which the newborn baby was surrounded by all manner of amulets designed to protect him against the evil spirits hovering everywhere about.

One source of superstition is suggested by Maurice Hindus in a memoir about his native Byelorussian village, where, as he recalls,

not only birds and beasts inhabited the wilderness but all manner of spirits, some as innocent and playful as kittens, others as cunning and cruel as hungry she-wolves. Though I never saw any spirits, I believed in them, for other boys and their elders had told of encountering them, of talking to them, of outwitting their sly machinations to inveigle mortal souls into bondage and damnation.... I especially feared yet was fascinated by the *russalka,* the spirit of a drowned girl who enticed boys and girls into her embrace, tickled them under the arms until they died from laughter, then dragged them down to the bottom of the river where she lived. Once I thought I heard a *russalka* laugh, the sweet melodious laugh that enchants the ears. My heart throbbed violently and I stood still hoping for a glimpse of the dazzling nymph—a girl with a deep bosom, big sparkling eyes, and long black hair flowing loose over her shoulders. Then I remembered that if I saw her she would bewitch me and I should be helpless to resist the fatal tickling. Panic-stricken, I ran crying out of the forest, not daring to look back until I was safe by the blacksmith shop in the clearing, where the presence of people, so ran the legend, would keep the *russalka* from appearing.

This particular legend was, of course, of Russian origin, and it had been picked up by the author from his *muzhik* playmates. It was as natural that this should happen as it was that boys should imitate games that they admired and that their non-Jewish neighbors played. But Jewish boys had ample resources in this respect in their own tradition. Morris Raphael Cohen traced some of his early fears of the supernatural to his reading of the volume called the *Kav Hayosher* in his grandfather's Hasidic house in the *shtetl* of Neshwies which filled his mind with tales of what *sheidim* (devils) might do to a little boy while he was asleep. It was a long time, too, before he could rid himself of his terror of the magical powers supposedly possessed by those who knew how to pronounce the four letters of the Hebrew alphabet that represent the real name of God, *JHVH* (which, according to scholars, ought properly to be sounded out as *Yahveh* and is identical with the English transliteration Jehovah). These experiences left the philosophical rationalist Cohen with a lifelong antipathy against what he called romantic obscurantism, though he had some admiration for the sounder aspects of the classical tradition of Judaism.

THE BATHHOUSES ON FRIDAY

Ablutions played an important role in everyday life. The Jew poured "fingernail water" in the morning, washed his hands before eating each meal, and had to pronounce a *berakha* (blessing) while doing so, in addition to the one he said over the meal itself. At the Passover feast, he washed his hands not once but twice; the second and sixth steps in the order of procedure at the *seder* involve washing of the hands. But the great ablution of the week was performed in honor of the arrival of the Sabbath. On Friday, the men, in company with their male children, repaired to a steam bath, while the women visited the ritual pool or *mikvah*.

Rebels against this custom no doubt existed among the youngsters who were subjected to it at all times, though the pressure toward conformity was so great that their true feelings were often not expressed till long afterward in retrospect rather than risked on the immediate occasion that provoked them. That it left some nightmarish impressions upon children is hard to doubt after reading a passage in Linetski's *The Polish Lad:*

Imagine for a moment that dark, burning-hot Jewish bath-house in Poland as it used to be.

There my father would cart me every Friday to the very topmost steaming bench where he used to scrub me with a brush for a quarter of an hour before the bath and for about ten minutes afterwards. And these two sessions were merely appetizer and dessert of the main dish itself! I mean the bath! The hard bristles were a torture, but the bath itself was terrifying. And it seems to me axiomatic that it is easier for a child to get over ten beatings than it is for him to recover from a single fright. Just picture it in your own mind— a three-year-old child, who knows only the beautiful outdoor world where he runs around from morning to night, and suddenly he is grabbed from behind, taken down thirty or forty narrow, crooked, broken, slippery steps into a cold, dark, damp hole where dozens of naked, soapy bodies are jostling one another for the least bit of breathing room—all of them grown Jews, you understand! Not little boys like me! Every sliding contact with their skins fills me with such horror as I can't possibly communicate. To make matters still worse, this scary experience takes place in a pitch-dark abyss. . . . At every other moment we can hear a distant flush of water followed by a piteous, stifled cry, like some dreadful echo issuing out of an impenetrable forest or some desolate wasteland, from which it will be impossible to extricate oneself. . . . And in the very midst of these gruesome proceedings, I suddenly feel myself grabbed from behind again and dunked into water completely, from head to foot! Coming up from under, I'm literally unable to tell what's happening to me or which world I'm in. Like a poisoned mouse, I grope around in the darkness trying to locate my soul again. . . . Whatever your imagination may suggest to you about such a horrible experience does not equal a thousandth part of the reality I lived through. . . . I shall not even bother describing the noisome odor of the place or the taste of the water, say rather slop! I became so spotlessly purified by these baths to which my father introduced me that to this day I am unable to cleanse myself properly though I use the most expensive soaps and the freshest water! And I've got lots of other reminiscences along the same line, though I realize very well that you will be inclined to treat them all as a joke. My father, however, did not think there was anything in the least humorous about the bath-house, nor I must confess did I. My father looked upon that steam-bath on Friday as the finest flower, the quintessential creation of the Jewish religion as he understood it.

Linetski is not unique in the substance of his complaint on this score, although his hyperbolic style has not been equaled by other writers and has made him, in the most authoritative opinion, a classic of Yiddish literature despite the fact that his name is virtually unknown to the American-Jewish reader. (Only a few chapters that I once translated have been published in English.) Mary Antin in her *Promised Land* has an almost startlingly parallel description (based, for all we know, on her memory of Linetski read aloud, since we know that he was a favorite in this respect among east European Yiddish readers of the period), in which she supplements the description of the women's steam bath with an account of the old-fashioned *mikvah,* a stagnant pool that neither looked nor smelled fresh but in which the women nevertheless had to be ducked a certain number of times in accordance with the prescription of a purificatory rite.

THE HEDER

Somewhere in the wide expanse of Jewish letters there must be softened, flattering, sympathetic, and nostalgic recollections of the east European Jewish *heder* (the most elementary Hebrew school), but it would be hard to find them. Not all writers, of course, are as vehemently satirical on the subject as Linetski or Mendele (who calls a Jewish school "a grave in which poor Jewish children are buried"). But even writers with the most positive attitudes toward every other aspect of Jewish life tend to draw the line at the *heder.* This may have been

because studies began very early (age three or four), the discipline was rigorous and punitive, and the hours spent there were inordinately long (nine, ten, or more). The poverty of the *mela-medim* (elementary teachers), the conditions of their homes, in which they had to carry on their instruction under the scrutiny of their wives, and the lack of esteem in which they were held —all contributed to the development of the worst sides of their characters. Shmarya Levin makes no bones about calling his initial instructor a sadist. He quotes a bitter folk proverb: "Two things it's never too late to do: to die and to become a melamed." There were three levels of teaching. In the first, the reading of a Hebrew text was taught but not necessarily its comprehension. In the second, *chumesh* (the Pentateuch) was studied, together with the commentaries of Rashi. In the third, the Talmud was taught.

Girls were spared the *heder,* since their duties in the Jewish religious life were so simple that they required no special training. But boys were a different matter. They were considered more important and less tractable, and there was only one way of dealing with them, it was thought. That was to put them, for the whole day, under the thumb of a *melamed,* who, if he had learned little else, knew the biblical adage about the consequences of sparing the rod. The school was a crowded room, lightless, and dirty. Shmarya Levin describes it as a kind of reformatory in which every child was looked upon as a young criminal until he proved otherwise.

Linetski in *The Polish Lad* presents us with a few unforgettable vignettes of *heder* life, as we might expect, laced with humor and etched in acid:

A long narrow table seesawed uncertainly on its legs. It was held together by ropes which were knotted over and over again, and its top was completely stained, burned and scratched. Around this table ran a "bench" constructed out of narrow, knotty planks of wood which were mounted on top of logs. Boys of various sizes were sitting on this makeshift so closely kneaded together they seemed to be a single doughy mass. One book served ten pupils, and the poor volume was swollen to three times the size it had been when it came from the hands of the printer.... On the very end of the table stood a big old basket and various pots, and next to these was a big tomcat whose tail, waving up and down with intense excitement, was whacking one of the smaller pupils on the head! In front of the room was a narrow doorway without a door. It was so low one could barely catch a glimpse of the lower part of the melamed's wife as she bent over to put something into the oven. Whenever the front door opened, she stuck her greasy face through the opening. ... Our melamed himself held the post of honor next to the stove. He never wore a coat, and around his shoulders was wrapped a prayer-shawl yellow with age. A cracked and mended skull-cap was perched on his head, and this yarmelke was so wrinkled with age and shrunken that it had only the faintest resemblance to what it had once been. It lay on his balding forehead like a great round mustard-plaster! In one hand he carried a stubby little whip, while with the other he scratched himself through his shirt, which was unbuttoned. One could catch a glimpse of the tangled growth of hair on his chest where he itched!

A jaundiced vision no doubt, but also one stamped with the unmistakable stigmata of reality and experience, and it is supported in essentials by virtually every other observer. Here, for example, is the same familiar scene painted by the poet Frug but this time freighted with irony instead of with the sarcasm of Linetski:

> Behold the palace, oh, how beautiful, how magnificent: ivory and velvet, silk, leather, bronze, cedar wood.... Here lives a Jewish melamed.... Of velvet is his skullcap—it glistens and shines from afar; the pointer is made of ivory; his girdle is of silk; the candelabrum is of bronze; the knout is of leather; the stool, o the stool is cut out of cedar wood!

Yet the poor *melamed,* if he were clever and had resources for rationalizing, could have made a case for himself, too. It was not his business or intention to make generations of little boys miserable, but he faced, under especially trying conditions, the ungrateful task of elementary teachers everywhere who are compelled to take from the young some of their natural freedom (a greater amount in this instance than is the case in some other cultures) and to break in the colt from his original wild disorderly gallop to the more stately trotting pace acceptable in a traditional society that sets a high premium upon conformity.

It was certainly a shrewd *melamed* who invented a little parable not merely designed to defend his despised vocation but to glorify it. There is a well-known Jewish saying that a man ought to respect his teacher as much as he does his parents. But who, among the many instructors one encounters in life, is to be regarded as *the* teacher who may lay claim to such honor, for it cannot be that every one of the numerous teachers is meant. This question, according to the *melamed,* was once brought to the heavenly tribunal for adjudication, and this was the answer received: the only teacher deserving the same honor as one's parents is the first, the one who teaches a child the *aleph beth* (or, as we should say, his abc's). And that is so because it is from him that we derive our greatest benefits. Later teachers of the Pentateuch, *Mishnah,* and the Talmud may have erred in their teaching or interpretation. Wittingly or not, they may have served to mislead their students. That is not the case with one who taught the letters and how to read from a text. He was never mistaken, and since the whole Bible is composed of letters in various combinations, only the first teacher lays down a secure foundation upon which others may later erect complicated structures more or less satisfactory. And this is the reason, he concluded, that a claim can be made on behalf of the humblest *melamed* that cannot be disputed by the greatest and most learned of rabbis.

The tale is a charmingly persuasive if innocently transparent sophistry, but it is solidly based upon what must be a well-nigh universal experience, namely that one's first teacher inspires feelings of either awe or affection that later teachers, no matter how distinguished, can hardly hope to equal. The idyllic picture it suggests, however, must be corrected with some realistic images of the squalor of an actual *heder* and of its overseer, who is anything but deserving of respect, not to speak of honor. Almost all who have treated the subject agree that the typical elementary *melamed* was either cruel or vindictive, lazy or ignorant, generally neglectful of his duties or unsuited to fulfill them, with little feeling for the importance of his work or any consciousness of respect for him by either parents or children. One may read Peretz or Abraham Cahan, Mendele, Shmarya Levin, or Linetski, the poet Frug, or an apologist for the Orthodox system of education in eastern Europe such as Solomon Simon, and accumulate masses of negative impressions that are mutually reinforcing of the *heder* as an institution. Though the world may have gone too far in the opposite direction now, the emphasis there was too exclusively upon the painful discipline of learning, which meant the utmost strain of one's mental muscles to master traditional subjects with traditional methods. A measure of success was attained by this rough-and-ready introduction to the exacting demands of the intellectual life—as the philosopher Morris Raphael Cohen attested—but it was purchased at a price that few who paid it thought, in retrospect, was worth it. There were some fine things, as we have seen, about the east European Jewish experience, but the *heder* was not one of them.

Hasidism:
Historic Roots
and Heyday

WHEN ONE THINKS of the east European Jew's physical appearance, likely as not the picture that will come to mind is that of a man in Hasidic costume whom one may have seen in magazine illustrations, on the streets of Williamsburg or Borough Park in Brooklyn, New York, or in the quarter of Jerusalem known as *Mea Shearim*. This is the image invoked by both romantic and satirist nowadays for the purpose of either lambasting the life-style of the contemporary American Jewish suburbanite or of trying to inspire him to another attempt at real religious renewal. In both instances, the attitude toward the Hasidic style and its symbolic medieval dress is highly laudatory, and it is suggested that they are signs of authenticity and integrity that are in sharp contrast to the modern faint semblances of the spiritual life.

Yet not long ago the fashion was to blame Hasidism for some of the darkest aspects of east European Jewish life: what the *heder* had come to, for example. We must recall that the alternative title that Linetski had given to his autobiographical novel *The Polish Lad* was *The*

Hasidic Youth. In doing so, he was simply carrying forward the earlier attitude of so-called enlightenment and reform with which the ethos of modern Yiddish literature in the beginning neatly dovetailed. And the philosopher Morris Raphael Cohen is expressing Linetski's point of view when he rejects the tendency of some of the less rationalistic modern philosophers who seek "to idealize the Hasidic combination of ignorance and superstition." Such falsification seems to him symptomatic of nothing less than "intellectual decadence and corruption."

To achieve some insight and perspective upon such radical differences of opinion and evaluation, it will be necessary to go back into history and consider whence the movement came and what, at the height of its influence, it represented. Hasidism was an impulse of religious enthusiasm that arose among the Jews of eastern Europe in the first half of the eighteenth century and has survived until this day, partly because a fragment of the movement in which it resulted emigrated to Palestine generations before the Holocaust and partly because another fragment of it escaped to America and elsewhere afterward.

A major part of the movement, however, undoubtedly perished in the early 1940s.

Those who have striven to make the characteristics of this movement intelligible to an audience familiar with a western European tradition have been inclined to find parallels between Hasidism and the Pietistic variant of Protestantism. Like the Christian Pietists, it is pointed out, the Jewish Hasidim assigned the primary place in religion not to dogma and ritual but to the sentiment and emotion of faith. Its aim, say these interpreters of the message of Hasidism, was to introduce changes into the believer rather than into his belief. By psychological suggestion, it strove to create a new type of religious man, who valued feeling above either reason or rites, and exaltation over precise knowledge and scholarship.

It was founded, we are told by these expositors, upon two basic assumptions. The first was a form of pantheism, insisting on the omnipresence of the divine power. The second was an assertion of the possibility of direct and intimate communion between God and man. Its principal initiator was the Baal Shem Tov (a religious title that is generally rendered as Master of the Good Name), who, like so many other influential spiritual and philosophical teachers in the history of mankind, was a purveyor of oral wisdom who never set down his teaching in writing and in fact is said to have denied on one occasion, when confronted with a supposed transcript of what he had been heard to say, that he had uttered even a single word attributed to him. Nevertheless, he is supposed to have instructed his disciples that man must continually bear in mind that God is always with him and that God is a subtle effluence everywhere diffused. In looking at material things, man must realize that he is in reality gazing at the image of God, which is present in all things. With this in mind, man must strive to serve God even in the most trivial matters, and he must do so with joy. This insistence upon identifying true worship with joy is one of the most notable characteristics of the movement, which at times shocked its opponents with the uninhibited quality of its dancing and singing and stimulated these expressions with a more copious consumption of wine and spirits than was regarded as quite respectable among Jews. Such indulgence was probably exaggerated by the opposition for polemical reasons, but the main thrust of Hasidism did seem to be away from rationalistic dryness and emotional asceticism.

Other interpreters of the meaning of Hasidism to the West have relied upon more fanciful analogies with the Romantic movement and even with American Transcendentalism. Frederik Schyberg, a Danish scholar who has written on Walt Whitman's poetry, has a curious conception of the Baal Shem Tov as a "Whitmanesque figure." The parallel he notes is the preference of both men for ordinary, elemental people: workmen and stage-drivers. He also speaks of "the notorious Hasidic cult of friendship for which the rabbi recruited young men from their homes and their work to follow him on 'the great highway' in the same peremptory fashion that Whitman used in 'Song of Myself' and 'Song of the Open Road.'"

Analogies are not hard to find if only one brings enough imagination to the task. Polonius, under the grim prodding of Hamlet, is able to discover a resemblance between a cloud in the sky and a whale at one moment and a weasel the next moment. To read back into the world of east European Jewry anything remotely resembling the American poet's "adhesive" love and "manly attachment" seems farfetched, to say the least. More natural and less forced is the tracing of connections between Hasidism and the vein of mysticism in Jewish tradition, which has been explored by Gershon Scholem. In line with this, an appealing hypothesis is that Hasidism may have been a benign development in response to the same situation that had produced the demoralization associated with the false messiah Sabbatai Zevi in the middle of the seventeenth century and its more malignant epigone, the Frankist movement of the eighteenth century.

The year 1648 is important in European history as the terminal date of the Thirty Years' War, but it has an additional claim to fame for those interested in east European Jewry. It marked the beginning of the Chmielnicki massacres, which may be looked upon as a preview of the Holocaust, and coincidentally it was also the year in which Sabbatai Zevi first made his claim to be the Messiah in the city of Smyrna—a declaration fraught with tragic consequences for the Jews lasting more than a century.

The massacres were touched off by the Ukrainian Cossack chieftain, Bogdan Chmielnicki, in conjunction with the rebellion he led against Polish landowners. As often before and afterward, Jews were caught in the middle between the summits of the social order and its lower depths, and the decade from 1648 to 1658 was filled with terror for them. In the vivid words of Singer's historical novel dealing with this period, *Satan in Goray*, "the rebelling Haidamak peasants spread havoc. . . . They slaughtered on every hand, flayed men alive, murdered small children, violated women and afterwards ripped open their bellies and sewed cats inside. Many fled . . . many underwent baptism or were sold into slavery." Towns once known for their Jewish scholars were completely deserted.

The number of Jews who succumbed in these atrocities has never been determined, but the lowest estimate exceeds one hundred thousand. Ninety per cent of those in the devastated areas who did not lose their lives were uprooted from their homes. A Jewish historian of the time is quoted as saying, after enumerating some of the horrors visited upon his people, that he will draw a veil of silence over the rest lest he bring the image of man into disrepute.

The messianic movement simultaneously launched among the Jews of Asia Minor meshed with this tragedy. Sabbatai Zevi, born in 1626, was early attracted to the Cabalistic mysticism of Isaac Luria, and, in the house of his father who was the Smyrna agent of an English trading firm, heard something of the expectations of Christian visionaries who had calculated that the year 1666 would witness the millennium. Prompted by Cabalistic calculations, Sabbatai Zevi launched his messianic pretensions in 1648, and between that date and 1665 the number of his adherents grew so sensationally that his name was discussed throughout large parts of the world.

The extent of his fame may be gauged from an extant letter to Spinoza from his English correspondent, Henry Oldenburg, the secretary of the Royal Society, dated December, 1665:

Here there is a rumor in everybody's mouth that the Jews, who have been dispersed for more than 2,000 years, are to return to their country. Few in this place believe it, but many wish it. You will tell your friend what you hear and think about the matter. For my part, I cannot put any confidence in this news as long as it is not reported by trustworthy men from the city of Constantinople, which is concerned in this most of all. I should like to know what the Jews of Amsterdam have heard about the matter, and how they are affected by such an important announcement, which if it were true would seem to bring a crisis on the whole world.

The reply of Spinoza to this missive, if there was any, has unfortunately not been preserved, but in his *Tractatus theologico-politicus* he grants the possibility that the Jews indeed "may, if the occasion presents itself amid the changes to which human affairs are liable, even raise their empire anew, and God may elect them a second time." If this was the opinion of a great philosopher, it is not difficult to imagine how vulnerable ordinary minds might be, particularly if they had witnessed cataclysmic disorders and epidemic destruction in eastern Europe, to the illusions and hopes raised by the millenarians of a new messianic kingdom and national restoration of the Jewish people.

Unfortunately for these dreams, the year 1666, which was supposed to crown Sabbatai Zevi's movement with triumph, saw his arrest on orders of the Turkish Sultan. Confronted with a choice between conversion to Mohammedanism and a painful form of martyrdom, the would-be Messiah of the Jews decided to embrace Islam. It is difficult to conceive of or to reproduce the disillusionment that this unforeseen perfidy produced upon the pretender's followers, most of whom felt suddenly duped and repented in haste of their gullibility. Those now old enough to recall the consternation produced by the Hitler-Stalin pact in the ranks of Communists and their fellow travelers in 1939 may have some inkling of what happened when the putative Messiah defected to another religion. Of course, as in all times, there was a hard core of Sabbateans who refused to believe in the evidence of their senses or else rationalized the betrayal and would not part with their illusions. It was this obstinate residue that later on created the Frankist movement (named after Jacob Frank, 1726–1791), which deserted the fold of Judaism for Christianity and played a smaller but no less disgraceful and confusing role in the eighteenth century than its predecessor had done in the seventeenth. But the bulk of those whom Sabbatai Zevi had misled returned shamefacedly to traditional Judaism.

The most pernicious effect of the messianic delusion was not the melodramatic departure to alien faiths by a comparatively small number of unbalanced extremists but the general disruption of the customary religious, social, and ethical fabric of the lives of many Jews who stopped far short of the brink of outright apostasy to the ancient faith of their fathers. Unchecked transports of emotion weakened the bonds of the old order and gave over the reins of leadership in many places to men distinguished by powerful feeling rather than directed by accuracy of thought. The more restrained and rational of the rabbis had difficulty in retaining authority long vested in them and resisting oracular mystics and upstarts. Social life was disrupted as it had been during the Crusades. The same popular radical, revolutionary, and prophesying types, who at all times thrive on misfortune, storm, and disorder, came to the fore. Precise grammatical studies and painstaking Talmudical exegesis, which were the mainstays of classical rabbinic Judaism, were abandoned by students in favor of the more heady intoxication of the Zohar and less well-known books of mystical speculation. The more self-respecting traditional scholars, whose conduct was curbed by conscience, were compelled in this atmosphere of confusion to withdraw for a time from their responsibilities or were forcibly driven from them. It was not for years that sounder stabilizing elements of the community asserted their control again and set about the task of salvaging what could be saved from the ruins of a wildly destructive period.

It was in the wake of the conservative, traditionalist, rabbinical reaction against the excesses of Sabbateanism that Hasidism arose in the earlier half of the eighteenth century. Like the messianic movement, it sprang from the Cabalistic current of the Jewish religion, but it made no fraudulent promises of instant national salvation, and it did not undertake to tamper with the basic traditions of Judaism or to relax the strictness of its behavioral codes. In fact, it tended to go in the opposite direction, particularly in the matter of the customary relations between the sexes, which the Sabbatean movement (and its Frankist offshoot later on) loosened up to the point of dissoluteness. No such imputation could be dreamed of against the Hasidim, for whom it was sinful even to look at a woman other than one's wife. Yet it had some of the same appeal as the messianic movement to the feelings of common men. Its emphasis upon song, story, and dance in religious ritual and upon the healing powers possessed by its charismatic zaddikim (righteous men) gave it widespread appeal and aroused the suspicions of the sensitized Orthodox leadership lest it develop into another form of antinomian zealotry.

The immunity produced by the reaction against the excesses of the Sabbatai Zevi movement caused the constituted leadership of the Jewish community to resist and, when necessary, to repress the eruption of Hasidic emotionalism in their midst. In Lithuania especially were the rabbis successful in their holding action (so that the word "Litvak" itself eventually became synonymous with *Mithnagid*—that is, a determined partisan of the rabbinical opposition to Hasidism). This opposition prevailed to the extent that Hasidism, though remaining a force and an influence in east European Jewish life for centuries, never rose above the level of sectarianism and was not absorbed into the Orthodox tradition in the way in which Luria and the Cabala were absorbed.

Authentic Hasidic tradition was preserved by disciples who were literate rather than literary, and it was left for later writers like Peretz and Martin Buber to build more graceful and aesthetic structures on the hints left by these amanuenses. Even a writer like Norman Mailer appears to have been intrigued sufficiently with the primitive elements of Hasidism to grapple with its fables, parables, and aphorisms in the pages of the magazine *Commentary*. The weaker side of the movement, which eventually led to

its decline, was its occasional attitude of anti-intellectualism. It distrusted, as much as did Rousseau and Wordsworth, the operations of the analytical faculty in man that "murders to dissect." It laid itself open, therefore, to the development of credulity on the one hand and charlatanism on the other.

But if trees were to be judged by fruits that had gone to rot, are there any that should escape being condemned to cutting down? The noblest creeds of mankind have never been proof against perversion, fanaticism, and deception. After the worst that can be said about Hasidism in degeneration and decline by satirists, rationalists, and critics, it must also be confessed that the movement has left a heritage of some value in melody, fable, and spiritual insight.

One of the most attractive figures in the history of Hasidism has always been Rabbi Nachman of Bratzlav (1772–1810), the great-grandson of the Baal Shem Tov, to whom Martin Buber devoted an entire book, because he was too large a figure to be fitted into the framework of Buber's two-volume study of the earlier and later Hasidic masters. The flavor of Rabbi Nachman's inspiration is contained in one of the little fables attributed to him, which has been deemed to have a theme similar to that of a famous fantasy of Kafka, a suggested comparison that turns out to be anything but discreditable to the eighteenth-century religious figure. This is Rabbi Nachman's imaginative invention:

Once upon a time there was a prince who was afflicted with the delusion that he was a rooster. He removed all his clothes, seated himself underneath a table, and rejected every form of food except corn seeds such as roosters eat. His father the king summoned many physicians and men of skill, but none of them could restore the young man to his wits. Finally, one wise man appeared who thought he could effect a cure and was given permission to try. He, too, took off his clothes, crawled beneath the table and began to munch on corn seeds. The prince was much disturbed, glanced at him suspiciously and asked: "Who are you, and what are you doing here?" His companion answered this question with an identical question: "Who are *you*, and what are *you* doing here?" The prince said: 'I'm a rooster!" The wise man replied: "So am I!" They sat there together until they had gotten used to each other, and when the wise man felt that he had gained a measure of the prince's confidence, he called for some clothes to be brought to him, saying: "Don't think that roosters can't wear clothes if they want to. We can wear what we please and still continue to be good roosters!" The prince, after pondering on this statement for a time, decided that he too would make the experiment. A little later, the wise man had food brought to him under the table, which alarmed the prince very much, but he was quietly reassured by his friend that roosters could consume the same nourishment as human beings without compromising themselves. Finally, the wise man said to the prince: "Do you think roosters must always sit under the table? We can get up if we wish and walk around." He suited his action to his words, and the prince, after thinking it over, joined him in his stroll....After he began dressing like a human being, eating like a human being, walking and behaving like a human being, the prince soon recovered his wits and began to live like a human being.

Lest the hearer miss the meaning of this pointed fable against the dangers of extreme nonconformity, the good rabbi, like Aesop, explicitly tacked on at the end the lesson he wanted him to learn: "Following the example of this wise man, a true teacher must get down first of all to the level of his pupil if he hopes ever to raise him up to his own higher level."

Who can doubt the real source of the power and persuasiveness of Hasidism, after appreciating not only the charm of this little tale but its genuine depth, psychological penetration, and profound knowledge of humanity? It knew its audience: its weaknesses, simplicity, suffering, and delusions. Hasidism encouraged its devotees to descend without condescension to the plane upon which the Jewish people were actually to be found in a given time and place, not for the purpose of exploitation but in order to raise that people to a realization of its full stature and potential for humane wisdom. Greatly creative rabbis like Nachman, the Bratzlaver (as he is affectionately known, after the name of the place in which he settled and carried on his ministry), covered over with the mantle of their authority the deficiencies of less gifted successors, who inherited the titles but not the inspiration, who admired the founding fathers of their movement but could not quite manage to emulate them, in purity of motivation, integrity of purpose, and sheer intelligence and charm.

The Place
of
Women

PROBABLY THE SINGLE most difficult transition for the contemporary reader to make into the traditional world of east European Jewry concerns the place of the women there. For purposes of comparison, let us begin with America. According to an extreme statement by Scott Fitzgerald in *Tender Is the Night,* "the American Woman . . . had broken the moral back of a race and made a nursery out of a continent." This is a description of how the matter appears to some observers in western Europe, where Fitzgerald might have acquired such a point of view. To Europeans, Americans appear to be little more than perpetual children, even without identifying the cause of the condition as what Philip Wylie called "momism." Long before the days of "women's liberation"—but long after the feminist movement had started—Fitzgerald had thought that it was American men who were really in need of liberation. In *The Beautiful and Damned* he tells us that America is the land "where ugly women control strong men . . . a melancholy spectacle. Women with receding chins and shapeless noses go about in broad day-

light saying 'Do this!' and 'Do that!' and all the men, even those of great wealth, obey implicitly their women to whom they refer sonorously either as 'Mrs. so-and-so' or as 'The Wife.' "

A Jewish visitor from abroad recently observed to an American conservative congregation that he thought that the most important innovation of American Jewry religiously speaking was, outside the Orthodox fold—daring to allow women and men to sit together during services. And, upon reflection, there is much to justify the observation. Even Herman Wouk, the staunch defender of Orthodoxy in America, is compelled to admit that both the Reform and Conservative movements have drawn a great deal of their power from their break with the age-old Jewish custom of seating men and women in different sections of the synagogue. In the Orthodox synagogue to this day, the men are seated in the conspicuous place, corresponding to the orchestra, while the women are either in the balcony, or, if there is no balcony, in the rear of the hall, which is partitioned off from where the men sit.

But the American Jewish woman, and more especially her daughter, like their American sisters of other denominations, find it hard to accept what looks like second-class status in any respect, and therefore the tradition of centuries has been compelled to yield. In the older east European community, the position of women was exactly what is suggested by the prayer said each morning in which the man thanks his Maker for the boon of having been created a man, while the woman in her own devotions simply expresses her gratitude to Him for having created her *what she is* according to His will. Again, we must go to Linetski for an extreme point of view. "Can you imagine," he asks rhetorically, "what the word *man* means to a Polish Hasid? A man—though he might in actuality be a stinking bedbug, a stammerer, and an imbecile—is still, among Polish Jews, the lord and master, judge and despot over the most intelligent, the most beautiful, the most talented, the most sensitive woman." That observation no doubt, like so many others by him, is colored by the savage indignation of the satirist, but it is a caricature that underlines an undeniable feature of its original model.

The Talmud extrapolates the original Creation story in the Bible by postulating that the original human being was both male and female and that God then separated the two halves so that neither is really complete without the other and each has to go in search of the other in order to restore the integrity of the original. It sounds very much as if the rabbis responsible for this idea had read Plato's dialogue *The Symposium* in which a very similar myth is propounded by the comic genius Aristophanes. Whatever its origin, the myth suggests a greater degree of equality and interdependence than actually prevailed in the culture of eastern Europe.

Religion was the cynosure of the community's attention, and man was at the center of every rite and ceremonial. When a child was born and it was a girl, there was a little sense of disappoint-ment. A boy, after all, was a *kaddish,* that is to say he would pronounce the prayer for the departed soul at morning, afternoon, and evening prayers in the synagogue for a full year after the parent's death and on all the anniversaries afterward. The girl's religious training, as already indicated, was minimal. She was barely literate, repeated Hebrew prayers by rote without understanding them. At best, she was a reader of Yiddish, the spoken language of the community, which, during a large part of east European Jewish history, was held in low esteem and referred to as a "jargon" not by outsiders but by those who used it themselves. A beneficial by-product of such an attitude was that girls were spared the rigors of the *heder,* but that was so only because they were deemed unworthy of the privileges to which those rigors led eventually. In a society in which whatever status and opportunity there were depended largely upon learning, it was hardly enviable to be excluded from its possibility.

The Jewish religion, like virtually all other religions, is mostly a creation of the masculine imagination, and while there have occasionally been women who played notable parts in it, they are on the whole as rare as are creative women in any of the arts. The older Jewish tradition accorded a full measure of recognition to this fact and to all the consequences that flowed from it. The arrival of a boy in the family meant responsibilities that were welcome burdens. There was, first of all, the *brith,* or circumcision, the sign in the flesh of his entry into the covenant with God. Then there was the *heder* and eventually, if he were intellectually capable of it, the *yeshiva* of higher learning. And at thirteen, there was, of course, the *bar mitzvah,* which was not today's gaudy affair to be sure but did constitute a signal recognition of a boy's importance by the community, for which *there was nothing corresponding in the case of a girl.* The institution of the *bat mitzvah* (the ceremony admitting the girl to the community that parallels the *bar mitzvah*) is a purely American invention.

Nor was the *bar mitzvah* for the boy the end of his Hebrew and religious education, as it is so often today. It was a relatively unimportant milestone along an arduous and continuing course. Learning, learning, and more learning to the limit of one's natural abilities and perhaps a little way beyond them—that was the rule and one had to be unfortunate, poverty-stricken beyond the norm, or an orphan to become an exception to it. And even in such cases, the possession of any discernible scholarly promise would take one as far as he could go. For one thing, there was the institution of *kest,* that is the custom of a bride's parents' making a commitment to a sufficiently studious groom that they would support him for a certain length of time (sometimes for years) while he went on studying without having to worry about supporting a family. Quite rightly it has been remarked that religious learning was the recognized route to upward mobility in the old country.

For a girl the real schoolroom was her mother's kitchen. Learning to bless the candles and prepare the *chalah* on Friday and to read Hebrew with a Yiddish translation was the minimal challenge; the more important task was to learn to bake and cook, to knit, sew, and embroider, and also (in some places) to spin and to weave. Still more urgent was it for her to be instructed by her mother in the religious laws regulating a pious Jewish household, particularly in those concerning *kashruth,* the rituals governing the proper preparation of meat and strict attention to various prohibitions against mixing dairy and meat dishes. Very early she learned that if her mother, in cutting up a chicken, found something amiss in it—some mark of injury or sign that the fowl had not been slaughtered properly in accordance with religious law by the ritual slaugh-

terer (the *shohet*), someone had to be dispatched from the house at once to the rabbi, who, after consulting his sacred tomes and examining the case attentively, decided what was right. If, according to his decision, the chicken was *tref* (forbidden according to ritual law), it had to be thrown out, even if one starved in consequence.

The years of freedom from care were very few. Though exempt from having to go to *heder,* the girl had to take care of the younger children (and the families were large) when she was little more than a child herself. And the burden of her own wifehood, alas, came only too early. One day she could be playing with her young friends and the next day be summoned to a conference with the *shadchan* (the marriage broker) who has had his eye on her for months and has been praising her domestic talents, piety, and looks among families with eligible sons. Everyone has approved the match but her, and this is her moment *for being appraised by her prospective in-laws.* If a girl, beyond the accomplishments already noted, could sign her name in Russian, add and subtract a little, and write a letter in Yiddish to the parents of her betrothed, she was considered well educated.

Of course, we may err in the direction of painting too bleak a picture. Girls somehow did learn popular dances like the polka, waltz, mazurka, and quadrille. In addition, without any training or ever having seen a sheet of music, they learned to sing songs in Hebrew, Yiddish, and whatever the language of the surrounding population was. Every girl had to have her ears pierced, for earrings were so necessary a part of her attire that even beggar girls had them. The adornment might be nothing more than loops of thread with glass beads strung upon them, but symbolically these served the purpose that jewels did for those who could afford them.

After marriage, no matter how early this came in her life, she was expected to be less concerned with vanities, and the first indication of this was the shaving off of her "crowning glory"—the hair from her head—and the substitution for it of a plastered-down artificial wig (or *sheitel*). It was a mark of real independence and rebelliousness on the part of a girl if she refused this ceremony of Orthodox loyalty, though many a woman who lived to become a matriarch and guardian of the traditional order began her married life with such an act of defiance. In any case, she was expected to assist her husband in his ceremonials whenever possible. It was she who prepared the cup of wine for *kiddush* on Friday night, had the *habdalah* candle ready for the ceremony of gathering *hametz* on the night before the Passover, lighted the memorial lights for the dead on the Days of Awe, prepared the feast of Passover (and all the ritual little dishes necessary for the ceremony) and the repasts preceding and following the fast of *Yom Kippur.*

Furthermore, in many cases, she either helped earn the livelihood of the family or was the chief earner. If her husband was a real scholar, the wife was almost sure to be the mainstay economically of the house. Women ran shops or they had stalls in the marketplace, or else they might help their husbands in the stores. Because of this participation in the struggle for existence, they did not live a sheltered life.

But however busy the woman might be and however indispensable her labors to the well-being of her husband and her family, she was still a dependent both psychologically and spiritually. The center of gravity in the culture was not the home or even the marketplace, where she enjoyed some kind of parity, but the synagogue, where she was at best a spectator and at worst an interloper. Being called upon so little in the ceremonies there and having so little knowledge of their content, it was natural that her attention should be so much distracted from the devotions that the women's section of the synagogue became proverbial for the tumult of talk there ("as noisy as the women's section of the synagogue" is a Yiddish expression). The "world to come" (*olam habo*) was not merely an expression in the *shtetl* but a fact in the mental life there that it is difficult for one today to understand fully. Therefore, the idea that the woman (although like all Jews she had a place reserved for her there) was dependent for any real distinction upon the faith, knowledge, and devotions of her husband must have been oppressive at times, (if he were sufficiently saintly and she sufficiently helpful, she might hope, as the saying went, to serve as his footstool in Paradise), no matter how generally resigned to her subordinate role she may have been. She could not but have resented, at least intermittently, the injustice of an eternal order in which she was condemned to play such a role, and if she was especially independent and rebellious (if she had dared, for example, to defy the custom of cutting off one's hair and donning the *sheitel* at marriage), she may even have had moments of doubt as to whether such an order actually prevailed in the "world to come" or wished it away if it did.

It is probably not accidental that among the immigrants to the United States, it was more likely that a hint of skepticism about the whole religious world-outlook should come from an Orthodox matriarch than from her husband. Indeed, in such a family the whole idea of emigration probably was supported by women more enthusiastically than by some men. Men who were sufficiently cautious went to the New World by themselves first in order to feel out the land and judge whether they could carry over into it the framework of observances in which they felt comfortable at home. Then they returned with unfavorable reports to the effect that it was difficult if not impossible to bring up children there according to their ideas of what a proper

Jewish life ought to be. And their arguments often prevailed until another outbreak of violence against the Jews (in 1905, for example) persuaded the woman to adopt a very "unwomanly" role and to argue persuasively that little Jews of doubtful piety were preferable to dead Jews and that they had to accept the first alternative as the lesser of two evils. Such a decision might eventually prove to be the salvation of whole family, but it is possible to sympathze with the patriarch's point of view as well as the matriarch's. Morris Raphael Cohen recalls that he was told by someone that, after he had begun to realize his early intellectual promise, his grandfather, who had stayed behind when the family emigrated, was heard to say that it had been the greatest mistake of his life to permit his gifted grandson to emigrate to America. And when the latter wrote the old man about the triumph he had scored in winning a gold medal from New York City for excellence in mathematics upon graduating from high school, his grandfather wrote back enigmatically but reproachfully: "Gold does not change its nature, unlike yourself!" For he had evidently heard that his grandson had given up saying his prayers and wearing his phylacteries each morning and had become like his schoolmates, a typical American boy who, like Huckleberry Finn, "don't take no stock in" old-time traditions and the immemorial customs of his ancestors.

Margaret Mead, in her introduction to *Life Is with People,* quotes with approval and regards as very significant one statement from a baffled woman turned up by the investigators who composed an interesting and significant portrayal of the life of the Jews in eastern Europe. Replying to questions as to what was thought in the *shtetl* on the subject of whether a woman possessed a soul in the same sense in which a man did, she said something like: "Women have *real* souls, but men have *recognized* ones!" It is at first sight difficult to decipher the precise meaning of this, because I suspect that the statement was translated from a Yiddish original. We are not told this, but it makes sense that the respondent used the word *emese* (from the Hebrew word *emeth,* meaning truth) where the word *real* appears, and the word *anarkente* for the word *recognized.* In that form, the statement really has a deep significance and expresses what the authors called a "feminist" point of view, which may have been unusual in the *shtetl* only in that it was so openly expressed. It is the statement of a thoughtful person with an epigrammatic turn of phrase, and the wit simply points up a truth about life in the communities of eastern Europe that places it in one important respect at quite a distance from the one that, for better or worse, has so long been familiar to us.

Radom Passageway

Street in Brody

Shops and Cellars, Brody

Doctor's Office

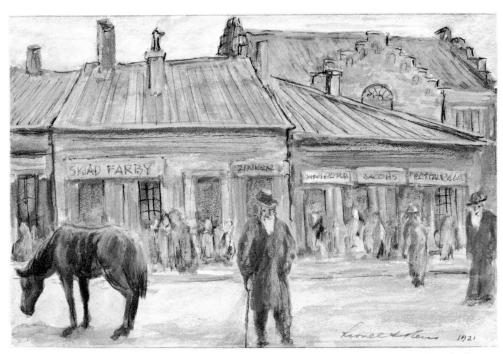

Brody Street

Passage Through Dluga, Warsaw

Polish Jew

Lublin Ghetto Street

Rabbi Meisel's Passage, Krakow, West

Przemysl Courtyard

Tinker's Shop, Lodz

KIELCE BALCONIES

Hasidic Dance

Tarnopol

The Virtuoso

The Piper

The Cymbalist

Beryl mit dem Bass

Blessing the New Moon

Polish Jew

Waiting for Work

Rag Alley

Firewood

Café Types, Warsaw

House in Warsaw

Transplantation

WHAT IS TERMED "the grand-father theory of history" suggests that, rather than progressing in a linear fashion, history moves backward and forward rather like a pendulum, since each generation reacts in some way against the one that immediately preceded it. And this reaction brings it near the position of its grandparents. For the same reason that no man is a hero to his valet, no parent can be a model to a child. But the same writer who noted the iconoclastic relation of valet to hero went on to say that the fault may be the valet's rather than the hero's. The same thing may be said of parents and children, and the "generation gap" is undoubtedly the source of much injustice on both sides.

But the position of grandparents is much more impregnable, especially when they live at some distance from the children, when they are sufficiently well-to-do to indulge them, sufficiently amiable to love them, and sufficiently dignified to command their respect. That is how it came about that in many immigrant families it was left to a grandfather, still scrupulously Orthodox but also Americanized to the extent that his beard was groomed as fastidiously as James Russell Lowell's, to bridge the chasm between the Old World *shtetl* of eastern Europe and modern America. He was capable of giving receptive grandchildren a taste for the tradition he embodied. A child of an immigrant mother whose own household was falling away from strict observance may still remember being lifted up to a big, old-fashioned telephone high on the wall on Friday night so that he might say the *kiddush* together with his grandfather. It was not quite the same thing as the festive welcome accorded to the Princess Sabbath in eastern Europe, but it was related pleasantly to that earlier world, and the Hebrew prayer that the child learned to recite by rote was the same as the one said by Jews there and everywhere. What the benediction meant he learned when he studied the Book of Genesis in Hebrew a little later on:

Thus the heavens and the earth were finished and all the host of them. And on the seventh day God ended his work which he had made; and he rested on the seventh day from all his work which he had made. And God blessed the seventh day and sanctified it because that in it he had rested from all his work which God created and made.

Such a grandfather might serve as the first rock of refuge to which to cling. The child admired everything about him and tried to imitate him in all his ways, as the Hasidim in the old country had minutely scrutinized and followed the pattern set by their wonder-rabbi. Though he was far from the most affluent, there could be little doubt that the grandfather was the most intellectual and aesthetic member of the family. He had an imaginative gift that naturally expressed itself in religious ceremonial and song. Naturally, he had committed the prayer book in its entirety to memory and never failed to don his tefilin (phylacteries) in the morning or to say his prayers three times daily as tradition required. He never sacrificed his convictions in the interest of expediency. He was a man of integrity.

A child seeking to imitate such a model could not but desire to become a *zaddik*, a saint, a holy man himself. The grandfather's gift was capable of making religion the most exciting experience in a young life. At *Sukkoth*, the child would help his grandfather decorate the *sukkah*. The nights of Passover were as thrilling as they had once been in eastern Europe, and the child sang the songs at the *seder* with such complete absorption that, although he was too young to be acquainted with the legend of Faust, if like him, the child had been asked to name the one moment in his life when he felt such complete enjoyment that he could have wished it to continue forever, even if he risked damnation for making the choice, this was the moment he would have chosen instantly and unhesitatingly.

Nor were the ascetic mortifications of the flesh on the fast day of *Yom Kippur* beyond such an impressionable child's spiritual reach. He might insist stubbornly on standing up throughout the services as only the most pious, bearded, east European-born rabbis in the synagogue did. In imitation of his elders, he would beat his little chest mightily for all kinds of nonexistent and indeed, to him, unimaginable sins during the ritual of collective confession:

May it therefore be Thy Will, O Lord, our God and God of our fathers, to forgive us all our sins, to pardon all our iniquities... [Such is the liturgical formula repeated over and over again on the Day of Atonement.]
For the sin which we have committed before Thee under compulsion or of our own free will. [Here he would give himself a blow on his chest with his fist so powerful that he could feel its reverberations inside his head.]
And for the sin which we have committed before Thee by hardening our hearts. [Bang!]
For the sin which we have committed before Thee unknowingly. [Bang]
And for the sin which we have committed before Thee openly or secretly. [Bang]
For all these, O God of forgiveness, forgive us, pardon us, grant us atonement.

It need come as no surprise to learn, in the light of this, that there were some children in immigrant households of the New World who had visionary experiences not unlike those experienced by their counterparts in the Old World. When, later on, these children grew up and, in reading the history of English literature, learned how the eccentric Romantic poet-painter William Blake confessed literally to hobnobbing with the angels and enjoying regular audiences with the Almighty Himself, the fact did not surprise them in the least. For they, too, knew what it was to have an imagination sown with religious symbols as Blake's evidently had been. There was no deceit, on one side or the other, in their grasp of the fact that inspiration is a part of both the natural and the supernatural orders of experience, an ambiguity that Blake tried to catch and communicate in his aphorism that "the Prophet is a man who realizes that the voice of honest indignation is the voice of God."

The enthusiasm and involvement generated by the religious instruction and ritual practices of Old World grandfathers were supplemented in an odd way by the superstitions spread by Old World grandmothers. If the clock struck the hour as someone was speaking, they said, it was an infallible sign that the person was telling the truth. The same thing might be said if someone sneezed. If one let one's eyes rest even for a single moment on the samite-sheeted *kohanim* (priests) as they were performing their devotions in front of the Ark of the synagogue that contained the Torah scrolls during a holiday, one was certain to be struck blind immediately for one's temerity. A similarly horrible penalty would be visited upon those who dared look directly at a flash of lightning, for it was during that very moment that the inner domes of heaven, which no human eye was ever supposed to see, were visible. The old women were also filled with stories about ghosts, about children who had been born with teeth (a sure sign that they were emissaries of the diabolical forces), and similar matters. The locale of all these tales was invariably the east European towns in which the families had originated and they had much to do with creating the earliest impressions upon the young mind of what it must have been like to live there.

Not everyone born in such a milieu cherishes nostalgic recollections of it. The painful part of the experience is evoked by a sympathetic non-Jewish observer, Lincoln Steffens, in his reminiscences of the days he spent as a reporter on the old Jewish East Side of New York:

The tales of the New York Ghetto were heartbreaking comedies of the tragic conflict between the old and the new, the very old and the very new; in many matters all at once: religion, class, clothes, manners, customs, language, culture. We all know the difference between youth and age, but our experience is between two generations; among the Russian and other eastern Jewish families in New York it was an abyss of many generations; it was between parents out of the Middle Ages, sometimes out of the Old Testament days hundreds of years B.C., and the children of the streets of New York today. We saw it everywhere all the time. Responding to a reported suicide, we would pass a synagogue where a score or more of boys were sitting hatless in their old clothes, smoking cigarettes on the steps outside, and their fathers, all dressed in black, with their high hats, uncut beards, and temple curls, were going into synagogues, tearing their hair and rending their garments. The reporters stopped to laugh; and it was comic; the old men in their thrift, tore the lapels of their coats very carefully, a very little, but they wept tears, real tears. It was a revolution. Their sons were rebels against the law of Moses; they were lost souls, lost to God, the family, and to Israel of old. The police did not understand or sympathize. If there was a fight—and sometimes the fathers did lay hands on their sons, and the tough boys did biff their fathers in the eye; which brought out all the horrified elders of the whole neighborhood and all the sullen youth—when there was a "riot call," the police would rush in and club now the boys, now the parents, and now, in their Irish exasperation, both sides, bloodily and in vain. I used to feel that the blood did not hurt, but the tears did, the weeping and gnashing of teeth of old Jews who were doomed and knew it. Two, three thousand years of continuous devotion, courage, and suffering for a cause lost in a generation.

Though this passage was written about the transplantation of human beings and their way of life from the Old World to the New, it could serve also with minor changes to describe what was happening in the Old Country itself in the decades prior to the Holocaust. For what Steffens was describing, whether he realized it or not, was the impact of the twentieth century itself and all it stood for, both good and bad, upon an ancient way of life. Increasing industrialization and technocratic triumphs, melting-pot types of democracy, Marxist panaceas and the totalitarian regimes to which their Utopianism was reduced in actuality, vicious and extreme forms of nationalism that cared nothing about the survival of any groups but their own, and the gravitational pulls in different and sharply conflicting directions that these exercised upon different elements in the Jewish communities themselves—all of these forces cast menacing shadows before them, as we can now see in retrospect, of impending disaster, unprecedented in Jewish history and perhaps in the history of the world, that was to be enacted in a few years during World War II on the soil of eastern Europe.

The world of the east European Jew is, in many ways, like all real worlds, so complex that, in attempting to depict it, one is continually attracted to opposite extremes. It is possible to oversimplify and to stress disproportionately one or two themes or strands in its structure. On the other hand, it is also possible to lose oneself and one's perspective in observations upon a great multitude of movements and impulses such as always characterize the texture of the historical process. The first type of fallacy leads to an immoderate emphasis upon piety and poverty, those Siamese-twin qualities of the life-style of east European Jewry over a period of hundreds of years. This may be called the sociological fallacy. On the other hand, what may be called the historical fallacy loses sight of the few basic patterns of a culture; it is easy, as the popular saying suggests, to see no longer the large outlines of the forest of movements and countermovements because we get bogged down in the contemplation of all of them individually.

It may be said with some justice that every "way of life" (in the sense attributed to this expression by anthropologists or as used in any of the social sciences) is only a manner of speaking, really a figure of speech. The trouble is that, while poets are aware that they are using figures of speech and therefore maintain to some extent a self-conscious detachment from the language that they use, social scientists are not always aware of the limitations of their own terminology.

No single point of view that I have ever read or heard about the experience of the Jews in eastern Europe before Hitler comprehends the subject completely, in my estimation, no matter how profound or intellectually or emotionally capacious its author may be. This is true of religious apologists and recorders like Heschel and Buber, of a philosopher like Morris Raphael Cohen, of historians like Dubnow or Lucy Dawidowicz, of Zionists like Shmarya Levin and Zalman Shazar, of Yiddish satirists like Mendele and Linetski and Yiddish nostalgic *baal teshubahs* (repenters) like the later Peretz, of a journalist like Maurice Hindus and a self-described *maggid* (or popular lecturer) and writer like Maurice Samuel, of a starry-eyed immigrant like Mary Antin, of gifted sociological anthropologists like Mark Zborowski and Elizabeth Herzog, of the variety of demographers, sociologists, and historians who cover the subject in *The Jewish Encyclopaedia,* and of the many many others who have written on the subject.

The complete truth about those vanished lives comprises all the accounts and many more that have disappeared because they remained oral and were never written down or else were written down and were cremated along with their authors. Walt Whitman said, after his own harrowing experience of nursing in the hospitals during the American Civil War: "The real war will never get in the books!" I am sure that the same thing can be said of the experience of any historical era. Our picture of it must of necessity be impressionistic and a little sketchy. The best we can hope for is that at least some of our suggestions may prompt the imagination of the reader capable of it to fill out what we have been compelled to leave fragmentary and perhaps also, by scattered hints, to indicate to him the many kinds of treasure troves of literary documentation that are there for the asking to be examined, and to encourage him, in the classic advice of Hillel in another and more august context, to go and study.

Chicken Market, Galicia

Market in Krakow

Home from Market

Outskirts of Przemysl

Ghetto Town Hall, Prague

Lionel S. Reiss

Rabbi Meisel's Courtyard, Krakow

Young Scholars

Bibliography

ANONYMOUS. 1959. *Children's Drawings and Poems: 1942–1944.* Statni Prague: Zidovske Museum.

ANTIN, MARY. 1912. *The Promised Land.* Boston: Houghton Mifflin. (After thirty-four printings, this book went into a second edition in 1969, with an excellent introduction by Professor Handlin.)

ARONSON, GREGORY, et al. eds. 1956. *Vitebsk amol: geschichte, zichronot, churbn.* New York.

BROD, MAX. 1963. *Franz Kafka: A Biography.* New York: Schocken Books.

BUBER, MARTIN. 1956. *The Tales of Rabbi Nachman* (translated by Maurice Friendman). New York: Horizon Press.

———. 1947. *Tales of the Hasidim: The Early Masters.* New York: Schocken Books.

———. 1947. *Tales of the Hasidim: The Later Masters.* New York: Schocken Books.

CAHAN, ABRAHAM. 1969. *The Education of Abraham Cahan* (translated from volumes 1 and 2 of *Bleter fun mein leben* by Leon Stein, Abraham Conan, and Lynn Davison). Philadelphia: The Jewish Publication Society of America.

CHINITZ, N., AND NACHMANI, SH., eds. 1962. *Slutzk and Vicinity: Memorial Book.* New York-Tel Aviv.

COHEN, MORRIS RAPHAEL. 1949. *A Dreamer's Journey.* Boston: The Beacon Press.

DAWIDOWICZ, LUCY S. 1967. *The Golden Tradition: Jewish Life and Thought in Eastern Europe.* New York: Holt, Rinehart & Winston.

DUBNOW, S. M. 1916–20. *History of the Jews in Poland and Russia,* 3 volumes. Philadelphia: The Jewish Publication Society of America.

———. 1927. *Jewish History: An Essay in the Philosophy of History.* Philadelphia.

———. 1929. *An Outline of Jewish History,* Volume 3, "The Middle Ages and Modern Times." New York.

GLATSTEIN, JACOB; KNOX, ISRAEL; MARGOSHES, SAMUEL, eds. 1967. *Anthology of Holocaust Literature.* Philadelphia: The Jewish Publication Society of America. 1967.

GOODMAN, PHILIP. 1970. *The Rosh Hashanah Anthology.* Philadelphia: The Jewish Publication Society of America. 1970.

GRANOWSKY, REUBEN. 1941. *J. J. Linetsky and His Times* (in Yiddish), introduction by Abraham Reisen. New York.

HESCHEL, ABRAHAM JOSHUA. 1963. *The Earth Is the Lord's* and *The Sabbath.* Cleveland, New York, and Philadelphia: World Publishing Company and The Jewish Publication Society.

HINDUS, MAURICE. 1938. *Green Worlds: An Informal Chronicle.* New York: Doubleday.

HINDUS, MILTON. 1969. *The Old East Side: An Anthology.* Philadelphia: The Jewish Publication Society of America.

HOWE, IRVING, AND GREENBERG, ELIEZER, eds. 1954. *A Treasury of Yiddish Stories.* New York: The Viking Press.

LEVIN, SHMARYA. 1929. *Childhood in Exile* (translated by Maurice Samuel). New York: Harcourt Brace.

LINETSKI, JOEL. *The Polish Lad* (a translation by Milton Hindus) of five chapters from *Dos polylische yingl,* printed in *Prism 2,* edited by Isaac Bashevis Singer and Elaine Hemley.

LIPTZIN, SOL. 1950. *Eliakum Zunser: Poet of His People.* New York: Behrman House.

MENDELE, MOCHER SEFORIM. 1956. *The Parasite* (translated by Gerald Stillman). New York: Thomas Yoseloff.

PERETZ, ISAAC LEIB. 1964. *My Memoirs* (translated by Fred Goldberg). New York: The Citadel Press.

———. n.d. *The Book of Fire* (translated by Joseph Leftwich). New York: Thomas Yoseloff.

REZNIKOFF, CHARLES. 1963. *Family Chronicle.* New York.

SAMUEL, MAURICE. 1963. *Little Did I Know: Recollections and Reflections.* New York: Alfred A. Knopf.

SHAZAR, ZALMAN. 1967. *Morning Stars* (translated by Sulamit Nardi). Philadelphia: The Jewish Publication Society of America.

SIMON, SOLOMON. 1956. *My Jewish Roots: A Personal Record.* Philadelphia: The Jewish Publication Society of America.

SINGER, ISAAC BASHEVIS. 1955. *Satan in Goray* (translated by Jacob Sloan). New York: The Noonday Press.

———. 1950. *The Family Moskat* (translated by A. H. Gross, Maurice Samuel, et al.). New York: Alfred A. Knopf.

SINGER, ISIDORE, ed. 1907. *The Jewish Encyclopaedia,* 12 volumes. New York: Funk and Wagnalls. Articles on a variety of subjects but especially those in Volume 10 on the history and sociology of the Jews of Russia and Poland.

VISHNIAC, ROMAN. 1947. *Polish Jews: A Pictorial Record.* New York: Schocken Books.

WIENER, LEO. 1899. *The History of Yiddish Literature in The Nineteenth Century.* New York: Charles Scribner's Sons.

ZBOROWSKI, MARK, AND HERZOG, ELIZABETH. 1962. *Life Is with People: The Culture of the Shtetl.* New York: Schocken Books paperback edition. The bibliography of this excellent study, which overlaps only in a few places the one I have compiled, will supplement mine and serve to guide the student interested in making further explorations in this field.

The little parable by Reb Nachman Bratzlaver is based on the translation made of it by Rabbi Jack Riemer in his article "Franz Kafka and Rabbi Nachman: Comparisons and Contrasts" printed in the April 1961 issue of *The Jewish Frontier,* the editors of which have kindly given me permission to use it.

Illustrations